CAMBRIDGE LIBRARY COLLECTION

Books of enduring scholarly value

History

The books reissued in this series include accounts of historical events and movements by eye-witnesses and contemporaries, as well as landmark studies that assembled significant source materials or developed new historiographical methods. The series includes work in social, political and military history on a wide range of periods and regions, giving modern scholars ready access to influential publications of the past.

History of the Pirates who Infested the China Sea from 1807 to 1810

Piracy on the coast of China in the nineteenth century inflicted chaos and serious economic damage, with large mobs of bandits attacking coastal villages as well as wreaking havoc at sea. Yung-lun Yüan's account of this period, published in Chinese in 1830 and in English in 1831, is a colourful depiction of the pirate scourge. Interwoven with the narratives of the pirates themselves as well as those of the courageous civilians who resisted them, the text describes the organisation and rules of the pirates as well as the authorities' attempts to broker peace. Also included is Sir John Dalrymple Hay's account of battling pirates in the 1840s, first published in 1849. Hay (1821–1912) describes his tenure as a British naval commander struggling to suppress piracy. As well as providing a naval perspective on the pirate problem, Hay recounts numerous anecdotes of daring and heroism on the seas.

Cambridge University Press has long been a pioneer in the reissuing of out-of-print titles from its own backlist, producing digital reprints of books that are still sought after by scholars and students but could not be reprinted economically using traditional technology. The Cambridge Library Collection extends this activity to a wider range of books which are still of importance to researchers and professionals, either for the source material they contain, or as landmarks in the history of their academic discipline.

Drawing from the world-renowned collections in the Cambridge University Library, and guided by the advice of experts in each subject area, Cambridge University Press is using state-of-the-art scanning machines in its own Printing House to capture the content of each book selected for inclusion. The files are processed to give a consistently clear, crisp image, and the books finished to the high quality standard for which the Press is recognised around the world. The latest print-on-demand technology ensures that the books will remain available indefinitely, and that orders for single or multiple copies can quickly be supplied.

The Cambridge Library Collection will bring back to life books of enduring scholarly value (including out-of-copyright works originally issued by other publishers) across a wide range of disciplines in the humanities and social sciences and in science and technology.

History of the Pirates who Infested the China Sea from 1807 to 1810

Yung-lun Yüan
Edited by
Karl Friedrich Neumann

CAMBRIDGE
UNIVERSITY PRESS

CAMBRIDGE UNIVERSITY PRESS

Cambridge, New York, Melbourne, Madrid, Cape Town,
Singapore, São Paolo, Delhi, Tokyo, Mexico City

Published in the United States of America by Cambridge University Press, New York

www.cambridge.org
Information on this title: www.cambridge.org/9781108029209

© in this compilation Cambridge University Press 2011

This edition first published 1831
This digitally printed version 2011

ISBN 978-1-108-02920-9 Paperback

The original edition of this book contains a number of colour plates, which cannot
be printed cost-effectively in the current state of technology. The colour scans
will, however, be incorporated in the online version of this reissue, and in printed
copies when this becomes feasible while maintaining affordable prices.

Additional resources for this publication at www.cambridge.org/9781108029209

靖海氛記

HISTORY

OF

THE PIRATES

WHO

INFESTED THE CHINA SEA,

FROM 1807 TO 1810.

———

TRANSLATED FROM THE CHINESE ORIGINAL,

WITH

NOTES AND ILLUSTRATIONS,

BY

CHARLES FRIED NEUMANN.

———

LONDON:

PRINTED FOR THE ORIENTAL TRANSLATION FUND,

And Sold by

J. MURRAY, ALBEMARLE STREET;

PARBURY, ALLEN, & CO., LEADENHALL STREET;

THACKER & CO., CALCUTTA; TREUTTEL & WÜRTZ, PARIS;

AND E. FLEISCHER, LEIPSIG.

———

1831.

L O N D O N
Printed by J. L. Cox, Great Queen Street,
Lincoln's-Inn Fields.

TRANSLATOR'S PREFACE.

CONQUERORS are deemed successful robbers, while robbers are unsuccessful
conquerors. If the founder of the dynasty of the Ming had failed in his
rebellion against the Moguls, history
would have called him a robber; and if
any one of the various robber-chiefs, who
in the course of the two last centuries
made war against the reigning Manchow,
had overthrown the government of the
foreigners, the official historiographers of
the " *Middle empire*" would have called
him *the far-famed, illustrious elder father*
of the new dynasty.

Robbers or pirates are usually ignorant of the principles concerning human society. They are not aware that power is derived from the people for the general advantage, and that when it is abused to a certain extent, all means of redress resorted to are legitimate. But they feel most violently the abuse of power. The fruit of labour is too often taken out of their hands, justice sold for money, and nothing is safe from their rapacious and luxurious masters. People arise to oppose, and act according to the philosophical principles of human society, without having any clear idea about them. Robbers and pirates are, in fact, the opposition party in the despotical empires of the East; and their history is far more interesting than that of the reigning despot.*

* The Chinese have particular histories of the robbers and pirates who existed in the *middle empire* from the most ancient times; these histories form a portion of every provincial history. The three last books (the 58th, 59th, and 60th) of the *Memoirs*

The sameness which is to be observed in
the history of all Asiatic governments,
presents a great difficulty to any historian
who wishes to write a history of any nation in Asia for the general reader.

The history of the transactions between
Europeans and the Chinese is intimately
connected with that of the pirate chiefs
who appeared from time to time in the
Chinese Sea, or Southern Ocean. The
Europeans themselves, at their first appearance in the *middle empire*, only became known as pirates. Simon de An-
drada, the first Portuguese who (1521)
tried to establish any regular trade with

concerning the *South of the Meihling Mountains* (see the Cate-
chism of the Shahmans, p. 44) are inscribed *Tsing fun* (10,987,
2,651), and contain the Robber history from the beginning of Woo
wang, of the dynasty Chow. The Memoirs only give extracts of
former works; the extracts to the three last books are taken from
the Great History of Yuĕ, or Province of Kwang tang (*Yuĕ ta
ke*), from *the Old Transactions of the Five Realms* (*Woo kwŏ koo
sse*), *the Old Records of Yang ching*, a name of the ancient city of
Kwang tung (*Yang ching koo chaou*), *the Official Robber History*
(*Kwŏ she yĭh shin chuen*), &c.

China, committed violence against the merchants, and bought young Chinese to use them as slaves; and it is known that it was the policy of the *civilized foreigners* from the "Great Western Ocean" (which is the Chinese name for Europe) to decry their competitors in trade as pirates and outlaws.

The footing which Europeans and Americans now enjoy in China, originated from the assistance given by the Portuguese to the Manchow against the Patriots, otherwise called pirates, who would not submit to the sway of foreigners. Macao, the only residence (or large prison) in which foreigners are shut up, is not considered by the Chinese Government as belonging exclusively to the Portuguese. The Dutch, on not being allowed to remain in Macao, complained to the Chinese Government, and the authorities of the middle empire commanded the Portuguese to grant houses to the newly arrived *Holan* or Hollander, "since Macao was to be considered as the abode of *all* foreigners trading with China." The edicts concerning this transaction are stated to be now in the archives of the Dutch factory at Macao.

It is one of the most interesting facts in the history of the Chinese empire, that the various barbarous tribes, who subdued either the whole or a part of this singular country, were themselves ultimately subdued by the peculiar civilization of their subjects. The Kitans, Moguls, and Manchow, became, in the course of time, Chinese people; like the Ostro, and Visigoths, and Longobards—Romans. But we may remark, that both the Chinese and the Roman civilization under the Emperors recommended itself to the conquerors, as connected with a despotism which particularly suited the views of the

B

conquerors. Though this large division
of the human race, which we are accustomed to call *Tatars*, never felt a spark
of that liberty which everywhere animated
the various German nations and tribes, and
the Khakhans, in consequence of this, were
not in need of any foreign policy to en-
slave their compatriots; yet it may be
said, that neither Moguls nor Manchow
were able to establish a despotic form of
government which worked so well for a
large nation as that of the Chinese.

The extremes of both despotism and
democracy acknowledge no intermediary
power or rank. The sovereign is the
vice-regent of heaven, and all in all;
he is the only rule of right and wrong,
and commands both what shall be done in
this world and thought of concerning the
next. It may be easily imagined, that the
Jesuits, on their first arrival in China,
were delighted with such a perfect spe-

cimen of government according to their
political sentiments. They tried all that
human power could command to succeed
in the conversion of this worldly paradise.
The fathers disguised themselves as astro-
nomers, watchmakers, painters, musicians,
and engineers.* They forged inscriptions†
and invented miracles, and almost went to
the extent of canonizing Confucius. But
this cunning deference to Chinese customs involved the Jesuits in a dispute
with their more pious but less prudent
competitors ; and notwithstanding all the

* We are chiefly indebted to the Jesuits that the Russians had
not conquered part of China about the middle of the seventeenth
century. See the passage of Muller in Burney's Voyages of Discovery to the North-East Passage, p. 55. The Manchow destroyed the Chinese patriots by the cannon cast by the Rev.
Father Verbiest.—Le Comte, Nouvelles Observations sur la Chine.

† We have a learned dissertation, pleading for the authenticity
of the famous inscription of *Se ngan foo,* by a well-known Sino-
logue. May we not be favoured with another *Oratio pro domo*
concerning the many crosses which had been found in Fuh këen,
and on the " Escrevices de Mer, qui estans encore en vie, lors
mesme qu'elles estoient cuites?" See Relation de la Chine par
Michel Boym, de la Compagnie de Jesus, in Theveno, et Relations
de divers Voyage, vol. ii, pp. 6 and 14.

cleverness of the Jesuits, the Chinese
saw at last, that in becoming Roman Catholic Christians they must cease to be
Chinese, and obey a foreign sovereign in
the *Great Western Ocean.* Toland affirms,
that the Chinese and the Irish, in the time
of their heathen monarch Laogirius, were
the only nations in which religious perse-
cutions never existed ;* this praise now
refers exclusively to Ireland. Roman
Catholicism is at this moment nearly

---

* *Toland,* History of the Druids, p. 51.—" This justice, therefore, I would do to Ireland, even if it had not been my country,
viz. to maintain that this tolerating principle, this *impartial liberty*
(of religion), ever since unexampled there as well as elsewhere,
China excepted, is far greater honour to it," &c. Never was a man
more calumniated than Confucius by the Jesuit Couplet. · *Confucius Sinarum Philosophus* was printed in the year 1687, shortly
after Louis XIV. abolished the Edict of Nantes, and persecuted
the most industrious part of his subjects. The Jesuit is bold
enough to affirm, in his *Epistola Dedicatoria ad Ludovicum mag-
num,* that the Chinese philosopher would be exceedingly rejoiced
in seeing the piety of the great king. " *Quibus te laudibus efferret,
cum haeresin, hostem illam avitae fidei ac regni florentissimi teterri-
mam, proculcatam et attritam, edicta quibus vitam ducere videbatur,
abrogata ; disjecta templa, nomen ipsum sepultum, tot animarum
millia pristinis ab erroribus ad veritatem, ab exitio ad salutem tam
suaviter (!) tam fortiter (!), tam feliciter (!) traducta.*

extinguished in China. To become a Christian is considered high-treason, and the only Roman Catholic priest at Canton at the present time, is compelled to hide himself under the mask of shopkeeper. In their successful times, during the seventeenth century, the Roman Catholic Missionaries published in Europe, that no nation was more virtuous, nor any government more enlightened than that of the Chinese; these false eulogies were the source of that high opinion in which the Chinese were formerly held in Europe.

The merchants and adventurers who came to China " to make money " found both the government and people widely different from descriptions given by the Jesuits. They found that the Chinese officers of government, commonly called Mandarins, would think themselves defiled by the least intercourse with fo-

reigners, particularly merchants; and that
the laws are often interpreted quite differently before and after receiving bribes.
The Europeans were proud of their civilization and cleverness in mercantile
transactions, and considered the inhabitants of all the other parts of the world
as barbarians; but they found, to their
astonishment and disappointment, the
Chinese still more proud and cunning.
We may easily presume that these deluded merchants became very irritated,
and in their anger they reported to their
countrymen in Europe that the Chinese
were the most treacherous and abandoned people in the world,* that "they were
only a peculiar race of savages," and required to be chastised in one way or
another; which would certainly be very
easy. Commodore Anson, with a single
weather-beaten sixty-gun ship, in fact,

---

* Toreen's Voyage behind Osbeck, II. 239, English translation.

set the whole power of the Chinese Government at defiance.

The Translator of the History of the
Pirates ventures to affirm, that the Chinese system of government is by far the
best that ever existed in Asia; not ex-
cepting any of the different monarchies
founded by the followers of Alexander,
the government of the Roman Prætors
and of Byzantine Dukes, or that of
Christian Kings and Barons who reigned
in various parts of the East during the
middle ages. The principles of Chinese
government are those of virtue and justice; but they are greatly corrupted by
the passions and vices of men. The
greater part of their laws are good and
just, though the practice is often bad; but
unfortunately this is generally not known
to the " Son of Heaven." It is the interest
of the Emperor to deal out justice to the
lowest of his subjects; but, supposing it

were possible that one man could manage
the government of such an immense empire, who either could or would dare to
denounce every vicious or unjust act of
the officers employed by government?
The Chinese themselves are a clever
shrewd sort of people; deceit and falsehood are, perhaps, more generally found
in the "flowery empire" than any where
else; but take them all in all, they rank
high in the scale of nations, and the
generality of the people seem to be quite
satisfied with their government; they
may wish for a change of masters, but
certainly not for an entire change of the
system of government.

There has existed for a long period,
and still exists, a powerful party in the
Chinese Empire, which is against the dominion of the Manchow; the different
mountainous tribes maintain, even now,
in the interior of China, a certain inde-

pendence of the Tay tsing dynasty. The
Meao tsze, who were in Canton some
years ago, stated, with a proud feeling,
that they were *Ming jin*, people of Ming;
the title of the native sovereigns of China
before the conquest of the Manchow. It
is said, that the whole disaffected party is
united in a society—generally called the
Triade-Union—and that they aimed at
the overthrow of the Tatars, particularly
under the weak government of the late
Emperor; but the rebels totally failed in
their object both by sea and land.

It has been falsely reported in Europe,
that it is not allowed by the laws of
China to publish the transactions of the
reigning dynasty. It is true that the history written by the official or imperial
historians is not published; but there
is no statute which prohibits other persons from writing the occurrences of their
times. It may be easily imagined that

c

such authors will take especial care not to
state any thing which may be offensive to
persons in power. There is, however, no
official court in China to regulate the
course of the human understanding, there
is nothing like that tribunal which in the
greater part of the Continent of Europe
is called the *Censorship*. Fear alone is
quite sufficient to check the rising spirits
of the liberals in the middle empire. The
reader, therefore, should not expect that
either the author of the " History of the
Rebellions in the Interior of China," or
the writer of the " Pacification of the Pirates," would presume to state that persons whom government is pleased to style
robbers and pirates, are in reality enemies of the present dynasty; neither
would they state that government, not
being able to quell these rebellions, are
compelled to give large recompenses to
the different chiefs who submit. These

facts are scarcely hinted at in the Chinese histories. The government officers are usually delineated as the most excellent men in the world. When they run away, they know before-hand that fighting will avail nothing; and when they pardon, they are not said to be compelled by necessity, but it is described as an act of heavenly virtue! From what we learn by the statements of a Chinese executioner, we should be led to form a bad opinion of the veracity of these historians, and the heavenly virtue of their government; for it is said, that one Chinese executioner beheaded a thousand pirates in one year.*

The author of the following work is a certain *Yung lun yuen*, called *Jang sëen*,† a native of the city or market town *Shun tih*, eighty le southerly from

---

* The Canton Register, 1829, No. 20.

† *Jang sëen* is his Tsze, or title. The numbers which are to be found on the margin of the translation, refer to the pages of the Chinese printed text.

Canton. The great number of proper names, of persons and places, to be found in the " *History of the Pacification of the Pirates*," together with the nick-names and thieves' slang employed by the followers of Ching yĭh, presented peculiar difficulties in the translation of *Yuen's* publication. The work was published in November 1830 at Canton; and it is to be regretted, for the fame of the author in the *great western ocean*, that he used provincial and abbreviated characters. I will not complain that by so doing he caused many difficulties to his translator, for a native of *Shun tih* would not trouble himself on that point ; but I have reason to believe that the head schoolmaster of Kwang tung will think it an abomination that Yung lun yuen should dare take such liberties in a historical composition. Schoolmasters have a greater sway in China than any where

else, and they like not to be trifled with.
These are particularly the men, who,
above all others, oppose any innovation
or reform ; scholars, who presume to
know every thing between heaven and
earth : and they may certainly satisfy every man, who will rest satisfied by mere
words. These learned gentlemen are too
much occupied with their own philosophical and literary disquisitions, to have any
time, or to think it worth their notice, to
pay attention to surrounding empires or
nations. If we consider the scanty and
foolish notices which are found in recent
Chinese publications regarding those nations with which the Chinese should be
well acquainted, we cannot but form a
very low estimate of the present state of
Chinese literature. How far otherwise
are the accounts of foreign nations, which
are to be found in the great work of
Matuanlin ! It will, perhaps, be interest-

ing to the European reader to learn, what
the Chinese know and report concerning
the nations of *Ta se yang*, or the *great
western ocean.* I therefore take an opportunity here to give some extracts from a
Chinese publication relative to European
nations, printed last year at Canton.

The *fifty-seventh book* of the *Memoirs
concerning the South of the Meiling Mountains,* contains a history of all the Southern barbarians (or foreigners) ; and here
are mentioned—with the *Tanka* people
and other barbarous tribes of Kwang
tung and Kwang se—the *Siamese,* the
Mahometans, the *French, Dutch, English,
Portuguese, Austrians, Prussians,* and
Americans. The work was published by
the command of Yuen, the ex-Governor-
General of Canton, who is considered
one of the principal living literary characters of China, and it consists chiefly of
extracts from the voluminous history of

the province Kwang tung, published by
his Excellency:—

The Religion of the Hwy hwy, or Mahometans.

" This religion is professed by various sorts
" of barbarians who live southerly beyond
" *Chen ching* (Tséamba, or Zeampa), to the *Se*
" *yu.* Their doctrines originated in the king-
" dom of *Me tih no* (Medina). They say that
" heaven is the origin of all things; they do not
" use any images. Their country is close to Tëen
" choo (India); their customs are quite diffe-
" rent from those of the Buddhists; they kill
" living creatures, but they do not eat indiscri-
" minately all that is killed; they eat not hog's
" flesh, and this is the essence of the doctrine
" of Hwy hwy. They have now a foreign pa-
" goda (*fan tă*), near the temple of the com-
" passionate saint (in Canton), which exists
" since the time of the Tang. It is of a spiral
" form, and 163 cubits high.* They go every
" day therein to say prayers."

---

* The cubit at Canton is 14 inches 625 dec. Morrison, under
the word *Weights*, in his Dictionary, English and Chinese.

By the kindness of Dr. Morrison, the translator had the pleasure to converse with a member of the Mahometan clergy at Canton. He stated, that in the Mosque at Canton is a tablet, whereon it is written, that the religion of the Prophet of Mecca was brought to China, *Tang ching yuen san nëen*, that is, in the third year of the period called *Ching yuen*, under the Tang dynasty, *i. e.* 787 of our era.* The compilers of the *Memoirs*, &c. have taken their extract from the historical work of *Ho* (4051, M.); they seem not to have any knowledge of Matuanlin, where the Arabs are spoken of under the name of *Ta she*. See the notes to my translation of the Chronicle of Vahram, p. 76. During the time the translator

* We see by this statement that Couplet is wrong in saying (*Confucius* Sinarum philosophus. Proemialis declaratio, p. 60): " Mahometani, qui una cum suis erroribus ante annos fere *septingentos* (Couplet wrote 1683) magno numero et licentia ingressi in Chinam."

was at Canton, there arrived a pilgrim
from Pekin on his way to Mecca.

The Fa lan se, Francs and Frenchmen.

" The *Fa lan se* are also called *Fo lang se,* and
" now *Fo lang ke.* In the beginning they adopted
" the religion of Buddha, but afterwards they
" received the religion of the *Lord of Heaven.*
" They are assembled together and stay in *Leu*
" *song* (Spain ?); they strive now very hard with
" the *Hung maou* or *red-haired people* (the *Dutch*),
" and the *Ying keih le* (*English*); but the *Fa lan*
" *se* have rather the worst of it.   These fo-
" reigners, or barbarians (*e jin*) wear white
" caps and black woollen hats; they salute one
" another by taking off the hat.   Regarding
" their garments and eating and drinking, they
" have the same customs as the people of
" Great *Leu song* and Small *Leu song* (*Spain*
" and *Manilla*)."

This extract is taken from the *Hwang*
tsing chĭh kung too, or the *Register of the*
Tribute as recorded under the present dy-

D

nasty (Memoirs, l. c. p. 10 v., p. 11 r.). I am not sure if *Ke tsew* (10,869) *keu* (6,063) *Leu song,* can really be translated by the words — *they are assembled together and stay in Leu song.* The use of *tsew* in the place of *tseu* (10,826) is confirmed by the authorities in Kang he; but does Leu song really mean Spain? The Philippinas are called Leu song (Luzon), from the island whereon Manilla is, and in opposition to Spain (*Ta Leu song, the great L. s.*), *Seao Leu song, the small Leu song.* It may be doubted whether *Leu song* without *Ta, great,* can be taken for Spain. The Chinese have moreover learned from Matthæus Ricci the proper name of Spain, and write it *She pan ya.* The Dutch, the English, and the Germans, are, from a reddish colour of their hair, called *Hung maou.* This peculiar colour of the hair found among people of German origin, is often spoken of by the ancient

Roman authors; as for instance in Tacitus, Germania, c. 4.   Juvenal says, Sat.
XIII. v. 164,

> Cærula quis stupuit Germani lumina? *flavam*
> *Cæsariem*, et madido torquentem cornua cirro?

It would carry us too far at present to
translate the statements of the Chinese
concerning the Portuguese and Dutch.
Under the head of *Se yang*, or Portugal,
may be read an extract of the account of
Europe (Gow lo pa) the Chinese received
by Paulus Matthæus Ricci (*Le ma paou*).
The Chinese know that the European Uni-
versities are divided into four faculties;
and his Excellency Yuen is aware of the
great similarity between the ceremonies
of the Buddhists and those of the Roman
Catholic church (l. c. 17 v).   The present
Translator of the "History of the Pirates"
intends to translate the whole of the 57th
book of the often-quoted Memoirs, and
to subjoin copious extracts of other works,

particularly from the *Hae kwŏ hëen këen lŭh*, or " Memoirs concerning the Empires surrounded by the Ocean." This very interesting small work is divided into two books ; one containing the text, and the other the maps. The text consists of eight chapters, including a description of the sea-coast of China, with a map, constructed on a large scale, of the nations to the east, the south-east, and the south ; then follows a topography of Portugal and Europe generally. Concerning England we find :—

The Kingdom of the Ying keih le, or English.

" The kingdom of the *Ying keih le* is a de-
" pendent or tributary state* to *Ho lan* (Hol-

---

* This statement is so extraordinary, that the Translator thought it necessary to compare many passages where the character *shŭh* (8384 M.) occurs. Shŭh originally means, according to the *Shwŏ wăn, near, joining ;* and *Shŭh kwŏ*, are, according to Dr. Morrison, " small states attached to and dependent on a larger one : tributary states." The character *shŭh* is often used in the same signification in the 57th book of our work. The description of the Peninsula of Malacca begins (Mem. b. 57, p. 15 r.) with the

PREFACE.   **xxix**

" land). Their garments and manners in eating
" and drinking are the same. This kingdom
" is rather rich. The males use much cloth
" and like to drink wine. The females, before
" marriage, bind the waist, being desirous to
" look slender; their hair hangs in curls over
" the neck; they use a short garment and
" petticoats, but dress in a larger cloth when
" they go out. They take snuff out of boxes
" made from gold and threads."

This extract is taken from the "*Register of the Tribute as recorded under the present dynasty.*"

" *Ying keih le* is a kingdom composed of three
" islands : it is in the middle of four kingdoms,

following words: " *Mwan lǎ kea* (Malacca) is in the southern
sea, and was originally a tributary state (shǔh kwŏ) of *Sëen lo*, or
Siam; but the officer who there had the command revolted and
founded a distinct kingdom." In the war which the Siamese some
years back carried on against the Sultan of Guedah, they always
affirmed that the King of Siam is, by his own right, the legitimate sovereign of the whole peninsula of Malacca, and that the
Sultan must only be considered as a rebel against his liege. The
statement of the Chinese author, therefore, corroborates the asser-
tions of the Siamese.

" called *Lin yin :** *Hwang ke*, the *yellow flag*
" (Denmark), *Ho lan*, and *Fo lang se.* The
" *Great Western Ocean* (Europe) worships the
" Lord of Heaven; and there are, firstly,
" *She pan ya* (Spain), *Poo keŭh ya* (Portugal)，
" the *yellow flag*, &c.; but there are too many
" kingdoms to nominate them one by one. Ying
" keih le is a kingdom which produces silver,
" woollen cloths,† camlets, *peih ke*, or English
" cloth, called long ells,‡ glass, and other
" things of this kind."

This extract is taken from the *Hae kwŏ
hëen këen lŭh*, book i. p. 34 v. 35 r; and
I am sorry to see that in the " Memoirs"
it is abbreviated in such a manner that
the sense is materially changed.

---

* On the *General Map of the Western Sea (Se hae tsung too)*
Lin yin takes the place of Sweden. I cannot conceive what can
be the cause of that denomination. *Lin yin*, perhaps, may
mean the island *Rugen ?*

† The common word for cloth, *to lo ne*, seems to be of Indian
origin; it is certainly not Chinese. The proper Chinese name is
jung.

‡ *Peih ke* is written with various characters. See Morrison's
Dictionary, under the word Peih, 8509.

" *Ying keih le*," says the author of the *Hae kwo hëen këen lüh* (l. c.), " is a realm composed out
" of three islands. To the west and the north
" of the four kingdoms of *Lin yin*, the *Yellow*
" *flag*, *Holan*, and *Fo lang se*, is the ocean. From
" Lin yin the ocean takes its direction to the
" east, and surrounds *Go lo sse* (Russia); and
" from Go lo sse, yet more to the east, *Se me le*
" (Siberia?). Through the northern sea you can-
" not sail; the sea is frozen, and does not
" thaw, and for this reason it is called the
" *Frozen Ocean*. From Lin yin, to the south,
" are the various empires of the *Woo* and *Kwei*
" (*Crows* and *Demons*), and they all belong
" to *the red-haired people* of the *Great Western*
" *Ocean*. On the west and on the north there
" are different barbarians under various names;

*   *   *   *   *   *

" but they are, in one word, similar to the
" Go lo sse (Russians), who stay in the metro-
" polis (Pekin). It is said that the *Kaou chun*
" *peih mow* (?) are similar to the inhabitants of
" the *Middle Empire*; they are of a vigorous
" body and an ingenious mind. All that they

" produce is fine and strong ; their attention is
" directed to making fire-arms. They make
" researches in astronomy and geography, and
" generally they do not marry. Every king-
" dom has a particular language, and they greet
" one another by taking off the hat. They
" worship," &c. (The same as p. xxx.)

My copy of the *Hae kwŏ hëen këen lŭh*
was printed in the province *Che keang*,
in the year 1794.

" In the narrative regarding foreign countries,
" and forming part of the history of the Ming,
" the English are called *Yen go le;* in the *Hae*
" *kwŏ hëen këen lŭh,* Ying ke le (5272, 6950);
" but in the maps the name is now always
" written *Ying keih le* (5018, 6947). In express-
" ing the sound of words we sometimes use
" different characters. This kingdom lies to the
" west of *Gow lo pa* (Europa), and was originally
" a tributary state to Ho lan (Holland); but in
" the course of time it became richer and more
" powerful than *Ho lan,* and revolted. These

" kingdoms are, therefore, enemies. It is not
" known at what time the Ying keih le grasped
" the country of North *O mŏ le kea* (America),
" which is called *Kea no* (Canada). Great
" *Ying keih le* is a kingdom of Gow lo pa
" (Europe.)* In the twelfth year of *Yung ching*
" (1735), they came the first time to Canton
" for trade. Their country produces wheat,
" with which they trade to all the neighbour-
" ing countries. They are generally called
" *Keang heŏ* (that is, English ships from India,
" or country ships), and there arrive many
" vessels."

This extract is taken from the *Tan chay
hëen këen lŭh*, and it is all that we find
regarding England in the Memoirs concerning the south of the Meiling Mountains (p. 18 r. v.). In the latter extract,
the author appears to confound the country trade of India and China with that of

* The syllable *lo* is not in the Chinese text, as it is supposed, by
a mistake of the printer.

E

the mother country. England is again mentioned in the notice regarding Me le keih (America), taken out of Yuen's History of Canton. It is there said, that the Me le keih passed, in the 52d year of Këen lung (1788), the Bocca Tigris, and that they then separated from the Ying keih le (p. 19 r.) At the end of the extract concerning the Americans (p. 190) we read the following words :

" The characters which are used in the writ-
" ings of these realms are, according to the
" statements of *Ma lo ko, twenty-six ;* all sounds
" can be sufficiently expressed by these cha-
" racters. Every realm has large and small
" characters ; they are called *La ting* cha-
" racters, and *La te na* (Latin) characters."

It is pleasing to observe that his Excellency Yuen had some knowledge of Dr. Morrison's Dictionary. In the third part of his Dictionary, Dr. Morrison has given, in Chinese, a short and clear notice

concerning the European alphabet. Yuen
seems to have taken his statements from
this notice, and to have written the name
of the author, by a mistake, *Ma lo ko*,
for *Ma le so*, as Dr. Morrison is generally called by the Chinese.

> *The Man ying, the Double Eagle, or*
> *Austrians.*

" The *Man ying* passed the Bocca Tigris the
" first time in the 45th year of Këen lung (1781),
" and are called *Ta chen* (*Teutchen*). They
" have accepted the religion of the Lord of
" Heaven. In customs and manners they are
" similar to the Se yang, or Portuguese ; they
" are the brethren of the Tan ying, or *Single*
" *eagle kingdom* (Prussia); in difficulties and
" distress they help one another. Their ships
" which came to Canton had a white flag, on
" which an eagle was painted with two heads."

This extract is taken from the History
of *Yuen.* I take the liberty to observe,
that the Chinese scholar must be careful

not to take the *Sui chen*, or *Chen kwŏ* (the
Swedes), for the *Ta chen* (the *Teutchen*)
In the *Memoirs*, l. c. p. 19 v., we read the
following notice on the *Chen kuŏ* (the
Swedes):

" The *Chen* realm is also called *Tan* (Den-
" mark) realm, and now the *yellow flag*. This
" country is opposite to that of the *Ho lan*, and
" a little farther off from the sea. There are
" two realms called *Sui chen*, and they border
" both on the *Go lo sse*, or Russia. They
" passed the Bocca Tigris the first year of
" Këen lung (1765)."

The Tan ying, the Single Eagle or Prussians.

" The Tan ying passed the Bocca Tigris the
" 52d year of Këen lung (1788.) They live
" to the west and north of the Man ying (Aus-
" trians). In customs and manners they are
" similar to them. On their ships flies a white
" flag, on which an eagle is painted."

This last extract is also taken from

the History of Canton, published by his
Excellency Yuen.

If we consider how easily the Chinese
could procure information regarding foreign countries during the course of the
two last centuries, and then see how
shamefully they let pass all such opportunities to inform and improve themselves, we can only look upon these
proud slaves of hereditary customs with
the utmost disgust and contempt. The
ancient Britons and Germans had no
books ; yet what perfect descriptions of
those barbarian nations have been handed
down to us by the immortal genius of
Tacitus ! Montesquieu says, that " in
Cæsar and Tacitus we read the code of
barbarian laws ; and in the code we read
Cæsar and Tacitus." In the statement
of the modern Chinese regarding foreign
nations, we see, on the contrary, both
the want of enquiry, and the childish

remarks of unenlightened and unculti-
vated minds.*

* It may be remarked, that Cosmas, about the middle of the sixth
century, had a better idea concerning the Chinese empire, or the
country of *Tsin*, than the Chinese have even now of Europe. Such an
advantage was it to be born a Greek and not a Chinese. Cosmas
seems very well informed concerning the articles of trade which
the Chinese generally bring to Serendib, or Serendwîpa (Ceylon).
He remarks, that farther than China there exists no other country;
that on the east it is surrounded by the ocean; and that Ceylon is
nearly as far from the Persian gulf as from Tziniza or China.
See the description of Taprobane, taken from the Christian Topography, and printed in Thevenot "Relations de divers Voyages,"
vol. i. pp. 2, 3, and 5. The Chinese about Canton have a custom
of ending every phrase with a long *a* (*a* is pronounced like *a* in
Italian) which is merely euphonic, like *yay* (11980) in the Mandarine dialect. If a Chinese should be asked about his country,
he would answer according to the different dynasties, Tsin-a,
Han-a, Tang-a, Ming-a, &c. *Tsin-a* is probably the origin of
Tziniza. It is a little strange that Rennel takes no notice of
the statements of Cosmas. (See the Geographical System of
Herodotus I. 223, Second Edition, London, 1830.) Is it not
very remarkable, that this merchant and monk seems to have also
had very correct information concerning the north-west frontier
of China, and of the conquest which the Huns (in Sanscrit Hūna)
have made in the north-west part of Hindostan? He reckons
from China, through Tartary and Bactria to Persia, 150 stations,
or days' journies. About the time of Cosmas, an intercourse
commenced between China and Persia.

YING HING SOO's PREFACE.

In the summer of the year *Ke sze* (1809),* I returned from the capital, and having passed the chain of mountains,† I learned the extraordinary disturbances caused by the *Pirates.* When I came home I saw with mine own eyes all the calamities; four villages were totally destroyed; the inhabitants collected together

* In prefaces and rhetorical exercises, the Chinese commonly call the years by the names employed in the well-known cycle of sixty years. The first cycle is supposed to have begun with the year 2697 before Christ. In the year 1804, the ninth year of Këa kïng, was the beginning of the thirty-sixth cycle.—Histoire générale de la Chine, XII. p. 3 and 4.

† The *Mei ling* mountains, which divide the province Kwang tung from the province Këang se. See Note in the beginning of the History of the Pirates.

and made preparations for resistance. Fighting at last ceased on seas and rivers : families and villages rejoiced, and peace was every where restored. Hearing of our naval transactions, every man desired to have them written down in a history; but people have, until this day, looked in vain for such a work.

Meeting once, at a public inn in Whampo,* with one *Yuen tsze*, we conversed together, when he took a volume in his hand, and asked me to read it. On opening the work, I saw that it contained a *History of the Pirates;* and reading it to the end, I found that the occurrences of those times were therein recorded from day to day, and that our naval transactions are there faithfully reported. Yuen tsze supplied the defect I stated

* The place where European ships lie at anchor in the river of Canton, and one of the few spots which foreigners are allowed to visit.

before, and anticipated what had occupied my mind for a long time. The affairs concerning the robber *Lin* are described by the non-official historian *Lan e*, in his *Tsing yĭh ke*, viz. in the *History of the Pacification of the Robbers.** Respectfully looking to the commands of heaven, *Lan e*

* I translate the Chinese words *Wae she*, by *non-official historian*, in opposition to the *Kwŏ she*, or *She kwan*, the official historiographers of the empire. Both *Yuen tsze*, author of the following History of the Pirates, and *Lan e*, author of the work which is referred to in the preface, are such *Public historians*, who write—like most of the historians of Europe—the history of their own times, without being appointed to or paid for by government.

Lan e gives the history of the civil commotions under Këa king, which continued from the year 1814 to 1817, in six books; the work is printed in two small volumes, in the first year of Tao kwang (1820), and the following contains the greater part of the preface:

" In the spring of the year *Kea su* (1814), I went with other people to Peking; reaching the left side of the (Mei ling) mountains we met with fellow travellers, who joined the army, and with many military preparations. In the capital I learned that the robber *Lin* caused many disturbances; I took great care to ascertain what was said by the people of the court, and by the officers of government, and I wrote down what I heard. But being apprehensive that I might publish truth and falsehood mixed together, I went in the year *Ting chow* (1817) again to the metropolis, and read attentively the imperial account of the *Pacification of the Robber-bands*, planned the occurrences according to the time in which they happened, joined to it what I heard from other

F

made known, for all future times, the faithful and devoted servants of government. Yuen tsze's work is a supplement to the History of the Pacification of the Robbers, and you may rely on whatever therein is reported, whether it be of great or little consequence. Yuen tsze has overlooked nothing; and I dare to say, that all people will rejoice at the publication. Having written these introductory lines to the said work, I returned it to Yuen tsze.*

sources, and composed out of these various matters a work in six books, on the truth of which you may rely."

Lan e begins his work with the history of those rebels called *Téen le keaou (the Doctrine of Nature)*. They were divided into eight divisions, according to the eight Kwas, and placed under three captains, or chiefs, of whom the first was called *Lin tsing*—the same *Lin* who is mentioned in the preface of *Soo*. These followers of the doctrine of Nature believed implicitly in an absurd book written by a robber, in which it was stated, that the Buddha who should come after Shakia (in Chinese called *Me lŷh*, in Sanscrit *Maëtreya*) is in possession of three seas, the *blue*, the *red*, and the *white*. These seas are the three Kalpas; we now live in the *white* Kalpa. These robbers, therefore, carried *white* banners. *Tsing yih ke*, B. i., p. i.

* The Translator thinks it his duty to observe, that this preface,

Written at the time of the fifth summer moon, the tenth year of Tao kwang, called Kăng yin (September 1830).

A respectful Preface of *Ying hing Soo,* from *Peih keang.*

being printed in characters written in the current hand, he tried in vain to make out some abbreviations; he is, therefore, not quite certain if the last phrase beginning with the words: "*Yuen tsze has overlooked nothing,*" &c. be correctly translated.

KING CHUNG HO's* PREFACE.

———

My house being near the sea, we were, during the year *Ke sze* of Këa king (1809), disturbed by the Pirates. The whole coast adjoining to our town was in confusion, and the inhabitants dispersed; this lasting for a long time, every man felt annoyed at it. In the year *Kăng yin* (1830) I met with *Yuen tsze yung lun* at a public inn within the walls of the provincial

* The names of authors of Prefaces, as well as of works themselves, which are not authorized by government, are often fictitious. Who would dare to publish or recommend any thing under his own name, which could displease any of the officers of the Chinese government? The author of the following Preface has a high-sounding title: " He, whose heart is directed towards the people."

metropolis (Canton). He showed me his *History of the Pacification of the Pirates,* and asked me to write a Preface to the work; having been a schoolfellow of his in my tender age, I could not refuse his request. Opening and reading the volume, I was moved with recollections of occurrences in former days, and I was pleased with the diligence and industry of *Yuen keun.** The author was so careful to combine what he had seen and heard, that I venture to say it is an historical work on which you may rely.

We have the collections of former historians, who in a fine style described things as they happened, that by such faithful accounts the world might be governed, and the minds of men enlightened.

* *Keun,* or *Tsze,* are only titles, like those of *Master* and *Doctor* in the European languages. *Keun* is, in the Canton dialect, pronounced *Kwa,* which, placed behind the family names of the *Hong,* or *Hing* (3969) merchants, gives *How qwa,* or *How kwa, Mow kwa,* &c., which literally means " Mr. How, Mr. Mow."

People may learn by these vast collections * what should be done, and what not. It is, therefore, desirable that facts may be arranged in such a manner, that books should give a faithful account of what happened. There are magistrates who risk their life, excellent females who maintain their virtue, and celebrated individuals who protect their native places with a strong hand; they behave themselves valiantly, and overlook private considerations, if the subject concerns the welfare of the people at large. Without darkness, there is no light; without virtue, there is no splendour. In the course of time we have

---

* I presume that the author of the Preface alludes to the *twenty-three* large historical collections, containing the official publications regarding history and general literature. I have brought with me from Canton this vast collection of works, which are now concluded by the *History of the Ming*. It must be acknowledged that no other nation has, or had, such immense libraries devoted to history and geography. The histories of ancient Greece and Rome are pamphlets in comparison with the *Url shih san she* of the Chinese.

heard of many persons of such qualities;
but how few books exist by which the
authors benefit their age!

This is the Preface respectfully written
by *King chung ho*, called *Sin joo min*,*
at the time of the second decade, the
first month of the autumn, the year *Kăng
yin* (September 1830) of Tao kwang.†

* See the first Note to this preface.

† In the original Chinese now follows a sort of Introduction, or
Contents (*Fan le*), which I thought not worth translating. It is
written by the author of the *History of the Pacification of the Pirates*, who signs by his title *Jang sëen*.

THE

HISTORY

OF

THE CHINESE PIRATES.

BOOK FIRST.

THERE have been pirates from the oldest (1 r.)
times in the eastern sea of Canton ; they arose
and disappeared alternately, but never were they
so formidable as in the years of Këa king,* at
which time, being closely united together, it was
indeed very difficult to destroy them.   Their
origin must be sought for in Annam.†   In the

---

* This prince was declared Emperor on the 8th February 1796,
by his father the Emperor Këen lung, who then retired from the
management of public affairs.—Voyage of the Dutch Embassy to
China, in 1794-5 ; London edition, I. 223.   Këa king died on the
2d of September 1820, being sixty-one years of age.   His second
son ascended the Imperial throne six days after the death of his
father ; the years of his reign were first called *Yuen hwuy,* but
soon changed to *Taou kwang—Illustrious Reason.*   Indo-Chinese
Gleaner, vol. iii. 41.

† Annam (Chinese, An nan) comprehends the country of Cochin-
China and Tungking.   There have been many disturbances in

year fifty-six of Këen lung (1792), a certain Kwang ping yuen, joined by his two brothers, Kwang e and Kwang kwŏ, took Annam by force, (1 v.) and expelled its legitimate king Wei ke le.* Le retired into the province Kwang se, and was made a general by our government. But his younger brother Fuh ying came in the sixth year of Këa king (1802) with an army from Siam and Laos,† and killed Kwang ping in a great battle.

---

these countries within the last fifty years. The English reader may compare the interesting historical sketch of modern Cochin-China in Barrow's *Voyage to Cochin-China*, p. 250.

* The origin of this family may be seen in a notice of Cochin-china and Tung king by father Gaubil, in the " Lettres Edifiantes," and in the last volume of the French translation of the Kang mŭb. Annam had been conquered by Chinese colonies, and its civilization is therefore Chinese. This was already stated in Tavernier's masterly description of Tunking, " Recueil de plusieurs Relations," Paris, 1679, p. 168. Leyden, not knowing Chinese, has made some strange mistakes in his famous dissertation regarding the languages and literature of Indo-Chinese nations. Asiatic Researches, vol. x. 271, London edition, 1811.

† In Chinese *Lung lae* (7402, 6866 Mor.); this name is taken from the metropolis of this kingdom, called by the European travellers in the beginning of the seventeenth century, *Laniam, Laniangh*, or *Lanshang*. Robt. Kerr, General History and Collection of Voyages and Travels, Edinburgh, 1813, vol. viii. 446, 449.—The Burmas call this country Layn-sayn ; " Buchanan on the Religion and Literature of the Burmas." Asiatic Researches, vol. ii. 226, London edition, 1810, 4to. The kingdom of Laos was conquered about the end of the year 1828, by the Siamese ; the

The son of the usurper, called King shing,
went on board a ship with the minister Yew
kin meih, and Meih joined the pirates, Ching
tsih, Tung hae pa, and others, who rambled
about these seas at this time. The pirate Ching
tsih was appointed a king's officer, under the
name of *master of the stables*. King shing, relying on the force of his new allies, which consisted of about two hundred vessels, manned (2 r.)
with a resolute and warlike people, returned in
the twelfth moon of the same year (1803) into
that country with an armed force, and joined
by Ching tsih, at night time took possession of
the bay of Annam. The legitimate king Fuh
ying collected an army, but being beaten repeatedly, he tried in vain to retire to Laos.

---

king, his two principal wives, his sons, and grandsons, amounting in all to fourteen persons, were cruelly killed at Bangkok. The
Protestant missionaries, Thomlin and Guzlaff, saw nine of the
relations of the king in a cage at Bangkok, the 30th of January,
1829. The First Report of the Singapore Christian Union, Singapore, 1830, Appendix xv. Is *Lang lae* a mistake for *Lih lae*,
which is mentioned in the *Hae kwŏ hëen këen*, p. 214? There
occurs no *Lung lae* in this work ; where the Indo-Chinese nations
are described under the title *Nan yan she;* i. e. History of the
Southern ocean.

Ching tsih being a man who had lived all his life on the water, behaved himself, as soon as he got possession of the bay of Annam, in a tyrannical way to the inhabitants ; he took what he liked, and, to say it in one word, his will alone was law. His followers conducted themselves in the same manner; trusting to their power and strength, they were cruel and violent against the people; they divided the whole population among themselves, and took their wives and daughters by force. The in-habitants felt very much annoyed at this be-haviour, and attached themselves more strongly to Fuh ying. They fixed a day on which some of the king's officers should make an attack on the sea-side, while the king himself with his general was to fight the van of the enemy, the (2 v.) people to rise *en masse*, and to run to arms, in order that they should be overwhelming by their numbers. Fuh ying was delighted at these tidings, and on the appointed day a great battle was fought, in which Ching tsih not being able to superintend all from the rear-guard to the van, and the people pressing besides very hard towards the centre, he was totally vanquished and his army destroyed. He himself died of a wound which he received in the battle. His younger brother Ching yïh, the usurper, King shing, and his nephew Pang shang, with many others ran away. Ching yïh, their chief, joined the pirates with his followers, who in these times robbed and plundered on the ocean indiscriminately. This was a very prosperous period for the pirates. So long as Wang pëaou remained admiral in these seas, all was peace and quietness both on the ocean and the sea-shore. The admiral gained repeated victories over the ban- (3 r.) dits; but as soon as Wang pëaou died, the pirates divided themselves into different squadrons, which sailed under various colours. There existed six large squadrons, under different flags, the *red*, the *yellow*, the *green*, the *blue*, the *black*, and the *white*. These wasps of the ocean were called after their different commanders, *Ching yïh, Woo che tsing, Meih yew kin, O po tai, Lëang paou,* and *Le shang tsing.* To every one of these large squadrons belonged smaller ones, commanded by a deputy. Woo che tsing, whose nick-name was *Tung hae pa,* the *Scourge of the Eastern Sea,** was comman- der of the *yellow* flag, and Le tsung hoo his de- puty. Meih yew kin and Nëaou shih, who for this reason was called *Bird* and *stone,* were the commanders of the *blue* flag, and their deputies Meih's brethren, Yew kwei and Yew këe. A certain Hae kang and another person Hwang ho, were employed as spies. O po tai, who afterwards changed his name to *Lustre of instruction,*† was (3 v.) the commander of the *black* flag, and Ping yung ta, Chang jih këaou, and O tsew he, were his deputies. Lëang paou, nicknamed Tsung ping paou, *The jewel of the whole crew,* was the com-

* People living in the same state of society, have usually the same customs and manners. It is said of the celebrated *Bucca- neers,* that they laid aside their surnames, and assumed nicknames, or martial names. Many, however, on their marrying, took care to have their real surnames inserted in the marriage contract; and this practice gave occasion to a proverb still current in the French Antilles, *a man is not to be known till he takes a wife.* See the Voyages and Adventures of William Dampier, and History of the Buccaneers, p. 87. Women cut the characters for common Chinese books; and, therefore, the Chinese say, so many mistakes are found in ordinary publications. The character *pa* (8123) in *Tung hae pa* is by such a mistake always written *pih* (8527).

† He called himself Hëo hëen (3728, 3676,) after having received a recompense from government for his robberies. See p. 75.

mander of the *white* flag. Le shang tsing, nicknamed *The frog's meal*, was the commander of
the *green ;* and Ching yïh of the *red* flag.
Every flag was appointed to cruise in a particular channel. There was at this time a gang
of robbers in the province Fo këen, known by
the name of Kwei këen (6760, 5822) ; they
also joined the pirates, who became so numerous that it was impossible to master them. We
must in particular mention a certain *Chang paou,*
a notorious character in after-times. Under
Chang paou were other smaller squadrons, commanded by Suh ke lan (nicknamed *Both odour
and mountain)* Lëang po paou, Suh puh gow,
and others. Chang paou himself belonged to
the squadron of Ching yïh saou, or the *wife of
Ching yïh,** so that the red flag alone was
stronger than all the others united together.

There are three water passages or channels (4 r.)
along the sea - shore, south of the Meiling
mountains ;† one goes eastward to *Hwy* and

---

* Our author anticipates here a little; this will be clear by a
subsequent paragraph, p. 13.

† *Shan* is a mountain in Chinese ; *Ling* is a chain of mountains
or *sierra*. The Chinese geographers say, the Meiling mountain

Chaou* ; the other westward to *Kao, Lëen, Luy,*

branches out like a tree; and they describe in particulary two, the south-east and the south-west branches from Canton. They speak likewise of Woo Ling, or five sierras, in reference to five different passes by which these mountains are divided; but there are now more passes. See a compilation, already quoted, regarding Canton, made by order of the former governor *Yuen,* and printed at Canton last year, 1830, in eighty books, under the title *Ling nan y ung shuh:* i. e. *Memoirs regarding the South of the Sierra,* book 5. vol. ii, p. 1.

* The Chinese possess itineraries and directories for the whole empire, for every province, and for every large town or place; I shall therefore always extract the notices which are to be found in the *Itinerary of the Province Kwang tung (Kwang tung tsuen too,)* referring to the places mentioned in our text.

Hwy is *Hwy chow foo,* from Pekin 6365 le, and easterly from Canton 400 le; one town of the second, and ten towns of the third rank are appended to this district-metropolis. The whole district pays 14,321 leang, or tael. Here is the celebrated *Lo fow* mountain. Lo fow consists really of two united mountains, of which one is called *Lo* and the other *Fow,* said to be three thousand six hundred *chang* in height, or 36,000 feet (?). The circumference is about 500 le. Here are the sixteen caverns where the dragon dwells, spoken of in the books of the Tao sect. You meet on these mountains with bamboo from seventy to eighty feet in circumference. Kwang tung tsuen too, p. 5v.

Chaou is *Chaou chow foo,* from Pekin 8,540 and easterly from Canton 1,740 le; eleven towns of the third rank belong to it. The whole district pays 65,593 leang, or tael. A tael is equal to 5·798 decimal, troy weight; and in the East-India Company's accounts the tael of silver is reckoned at six shillings and eight-pence sterling. *Foo* is the Chinese name for the first class of towns; *Chow* for the second, *Hëen* for the third. I sometimes have translated *Chow* by district-town, and *Hëen* by borough, or market-town.

CHINESE PIRATES. 9

Këung, Kin, Tan, Yae and *Wan;** and a third between these two, to *Kwang* and *Chow.*† The

* *Kaou* is *Kaou chow foo*, from Pekin 7,767, north-west from Canton 930 le; the district, and five towns of the third class, paying together 62,566 leang, are dependent on the district-metropolis.

Lëen is *Lëen chow foo*, from Pekin 9,065, from Canton 1,515 le; the district and two towns, paying together 1,681 leang, are dependent on the district-metropolis.

Luy is *Luy chow foo*, from Pekin 8,210, westerly from Canton 1,380 le; the district and its towns, paying together 13,706 leang, are dependent on the district-metropolis.

Këung is *Këung chow foo*, the capital of the island *Hae nan* or Hainan, from Pekin 9,690, south-west from Canton 1,680 le; three district towns, and ten towns of the third class, paying together 89,447 leang, are dependent on this capital. There is a town also called *Këung shan hëen*, and both town and capital take their name from the mountain *Këung*.

Kin is *Kin chow*, dependent on *Lëen chow foo*, and far from it 140 le.

Tan is *Tan chow*, a town of Hainan, south-west from the capital 370 le; the area of the town is 31 le.

Yae is *Yae chow*, a town of Hainan, southerly from the capital of the island 1,114 le. About this town many pirates have their lurking-place. This circumstance may have caused the mistake of Captain Krusenstern, stating that in A.D. 1805, the pirates who infest the coast of China had obtained possession of the whole island of Hainan.

Wan is *Wan chow*, a town of Hainan, in a south-easterly direction from the capital of the island 470 le.

† *Kwang* is *Kwang tung sång*, or the metropolis of the province Kwang tung (Canton). Ten departments (foo), nine districts (chow), and seventy-eight towns of the third class (hëen), are dependent on the provincial city, and pay together in land-tax 1,272,696 leang, excise 47,510 leang, and in other miscellaneous taxes

H

ocean surrounds these passages, and here trading vessels from all the world meet together,
wherefore this track is called " *The great meet-*

5,990 leang. The import duties from the sea-side with measure-
ment of foreign vessels is said in the *Kwang tung tsuen too*,
p. 3v, to amonnt to 43,750 leang. All duties together of the
province of Canton amount to 1,369,946 taels, about £450,000.
The lists of population gave last October (1830) 23,000,000 (?)
for the whole province, and we now see that the Chinese pay
less duties (every inhabitant about fourpence halfpenny) than
the population of any country of Europe. I received the population lists from *Ahong*, an intelligent Chinese, well known to the
English residents at Canton. Distance from Pekin about 6,835 le.

The subject concerning the population of China, and the
amount of the *land-rent*, the *poll-tax*, and other miscellaneous
taxes, is surrounded by so many difficulties, that the writer of this
dares not to affirm any thing about these matters until he has
perused the new edition of *Tay tsing hwy tëen*. For the present
he will merely remark, that in book 141, p. 38, of the said work,
the population of China Proper for the year 1793 is reckoned
at 307,467,200. If we add to this number the population of
Chinese Tartary, it will certainly amount to the round number
of 333,000,000, as reported by Lord Macartney.

Chow is *chow king foo*, from Pekin about 4,720, north-west from
Canton 360 le. There is certainly some mistake in the Chinese
Itinerary; how could Canton be only 6,835, and Chow king foo
7420 le? The imperial edition of the Tay tsing hwy tëen (book
122, p. 6 v.) only gives 5,494 le as the distance from Canton
to Pekin; there seems to be a different sort of le. The district
and eleven towns of the third class, paying together 162,392 leang
depend on the district metropolis.

With the aid of the Chinese Itineraries and the new edition of
the *Tay tsing hwy tëen* (printed 1797, in 360 large volumes) it would
be an easy task to compile a " Chinese Gazetteer."

ing from the east and the south." The piratical
squadrons dividing between them the water
passages and the adjoining coasts, robbed and
carried away all that fell into their hands. Both
the eastern and the middle passage have been
retained by the three piratical squadrons, Ching
yĭh saou, O po tae, and Leang paou ; the western
passage was under the three others, nicknamed
Bird and stone, Frog's meal, and *the Scourge of the* (4 v.)
eastern sea. Peace and quietness was not
known by the inhabitants of the sea-coast for
a period of ten years. On the side from *Wei
chow* and *Neaou chow* * farther on to the sea, the
passage was totally cut off; scarcely any man
came hither. In this direction is a small island,
surrounded on all sides by high mountains,
where in stormy weather a hundred vessels
find a safe anchorage ; here the pirates retired
when they could not commit any robberies.
This land contains fine paddy fields, and abounds
in all kinds of animals, flowers, and fruits. This

---

* I found no particulars concerning these two small *islands*
(Chow signifies island) in the Canton Itinerary; and I looked in
vain on the great map of the Chinese sea-coast in the Hae kwŏ
hëen këen for their position.

island was the lurking-place of the robbers,
where they stayed and prepared all the stores
for their shipping.

(5 r.)   Chang paou was a native of Sin hwy, near the
mouth of the river,* and the son of a fisherman.
Being fifteen years of age, he went with his
father a fishing in the sea, and they were consequently taken prisoners by Ching yĭh, who
roamed about the mouth of the river, ravaging
and plundering.   Ching yĭh saw Paou, and
liked him so much, that he could not depart
from him.   Paou was indeed a clever fellow—he
managed all business very well; being also a
fine young man, he became a favourite of Ching
yĭh,† and was made a head-man or captain.   It
happened, that on the seventeenth day of the
tenth moon, in the twentieth year of Këa king
1807. (about the end of 1807), Ching yĭh perished in

* The town *Sin hwy* is south-west from Canton 230 le ; its
area is 138 le (?) and the taxes amount to 28,607 leang. This place
suffered much from the pirates.   I find no proper name for the
river on which Sin hwy lies in the Chinese maps, it is merely
called *Këang*, river.   Near this place is the island where the
last emperor of the Sung cast himself into the sea (1280).

† The word *pe* (8335) cannot be translated in any European
language.   It means a vice common in Asia.

a heavy gale, and his legitimate wife *Shĭh* 1807.
placed the whole crew under the sway of Paou ;
but so that she herself should be considered
the Commander of all the squadrons together,—
for this reason the division Ching yih was then (5 v.)
called *Ching yĭh saou*, or *the wife of Ching
yĭh.** Being chief captain, Paou robbed and
plundered incessantly, and daily increased his
men and his vessels. He made the three following regulations :—

First :

*If any man goes privately on shore, or what
is called transgressing the bars, he shall be
taken and his ears be perforated in the presence of
the whole fleet ; repeating the same act, he shall
suffer death.*

Second :

*Not the least thing shall be taken privately from
the stolen and plundered goods. All shall be re-
gistered, and the pirate receive for himself, out of*

---

* The pirates probably made use of the term *saou* (8833) and
not of *tse* (10575), because *saou* written with a different character
(8834), is the general term for boats and ships. *Paou* must be
considered as the lieutenant or first minister of Mistress *Ching*,
she being herself of the family *Shĭh*.

1807. *ten parts, only two; eight parts belong to the store-*
house, called the general fund; taking any thing
out of this general fund, without permission, shall
be death.

Third:

No person shall debauch at his pleasure captive
women taken in the villages and open places, and
(6 r.) *brought on board a ship; he must first request the*
ship's purser for permission, and then go aside in
the ship's hold. To use violence against any woman,
or to wed her without permission, shall be punished
*with death.**

That the pirates might never feel want of provisions, Chang paou gained the country people
to their interest. It was ordered, that wine, rice,
and all other goods, should be paid for to the
villagers; it was made capital punishment to
take any thing of this kind by force or without
paying for it. For this reason the pirates were
never in want of gunpowder, provisions, and all

* It will be very interesting to compare the regulations of Paou
with those of the Buccaneers. When these pirates had got a considerable booty, each person, holding up his hand, solemnly pro-
tested that he had secreted nothing of what he had taken.—Voyage, l. c. p. 95.

other necessaries.   By this strong discipline the 1807 whole crew of the fleet was kept in order.

The wife of Ching yïh was very strict in every transaction; nothing could be done without a written application.   Anything which had been taken, or plundered, was regularly entered on the register of the storehouse.   The pirates received out of this common fund what they were in need of, and nobody dared to have private (6 v.) possessions.   If on a piratical expedition any man left the line of battle, whether by advancing or receding, every pirate might accuse him at a general meeting, and on being found guilty, he was beheaded.   Knowing how watchful Chang paou was on every side, the pirates took great care to behave themselves well.

The pirates used to call the purser, or secretary of the storehouse, *Ink and writing master* ; and they called their piratical plunder only *a transhipping of goods.*

There was a temple in *Hwy chow* dedicated to the *spirits of the three mothers,** near the sea-

---

† The *San po* (8788, 8608) are national spirits, and, as it seems, not connected with Buddhism; there is a great variety in the

1807. coast, and many came thither to worship. The pirates visited this place whenever they passed it with their vessels, pretending to worship; but this was not the case—they thought of mischief, and had only their business to attend. Once they came with the commander at their head, as if to worship, but they laid hold on the image or statue to take it away. They tried in vain from morning to the evening,—they were all (7 r.) together not able to move it. Chang paou alone† was able to raise the image, and being a fair wind, he gave order to bring it on board a ship. All who were concerned in this transaction feared to find, from the wrath of the spirit, their death in the piratical expeditions. They all prayed to escape the vengeance of heaven.

1808.   On the seventh moon of the thirteenth year,

---

number of these good old mothers, who by the different emperors have been declared saints, or spirits, for the Emperor of China is likewise the pope in his empire. Dr. Morrison has an interesting article on these old women in his Canton Vocabulary. *Kang he* mentions only two *Po* (s. v.), who may be considered as spirits. This is a character of which the Buddhists are very fond; perhaps the translator may be wrong, and that *San po* is merely the Sanscrit word *Swayam-bhú*.

‡ Our author shews every where his partiality for Chang paou.

the naval officer of the garrison at the Bocca 1808.
Tigris,* Kwŏ lang lin, sailed into the sea to fight
the pirates. Chang paou was informed by his
spies of this officer's arrival, and prepared an
ambush in a sequestered bay. He met Kwŏ lang
on a false attack, with a few vessels only ; but
twenty-five vessels came from behind, and the
pirates surrounded Kwŏ lang's squadron in three (7 v.)
lines near Ma chow yang.‡ There followed a
fierce battle, which lasted from the morning to
the evening; it was impossible for Kwŏ lang to
break through the enemy's lines, and he determined to die fighting. Paou advanced ; but
Lang fought exceedingly hard against him. He
loaded a gun and fired it at Paou, who perceiv-

---

* The author said just before that the dominion of the pirates
in the Chinese sea lasted about ten years ; but he only describes
the transactions of the last three years, when their power and
strength was at the highest point. He begins to give particulars
from the 7th moon of the 13th year of Këa king, which corresponds nearly to the beginning of September 1808.

† There are three wretched forts at the Hoo mun, the mouth of
the Canton river, which could scarcely hinder any European vessel
from passing through.

‡ One of the islands marked upon European maps is called
The Ladrones : these Ladrones, so called from the pirates, have
all particular names on Chinese maps.

I

1808. ing the gun directed against him, gave way.
Seeing this, the people thought he was wounded
and dying; but as soon as the smoke vanished
Paou stood again firm and upright, so that all
thought he was a spirit. The pirates instantly
grappled Kwŏ lang's ship; Paou was the fore-
most, and Leang po paou the first to mount
the vessel; he killed the helmsman, and took
the ship. The pirates crowded about; the
commander Kwŏ lang engaging with small
arms, much blood was shed. This murderous
(8 r.) battle lasted till night time; the bodies of the
dead surrounded the vessels on all sides, and
there perished an immense number of the pirates.
Between three and five o'clock the pirates had
destroyed or sunk three of our vessels. The other
officers of Kwŏ being afraid that they also might
perish in the sea, displayed not all their strength;
so it happened that the pirates making a sudden
attack, captured the whole remaining fifteen
vessels. Paou wished very much that Kwŏ
lang would surrender, but Lang becoming
desperate, suddenly seized the pirate by
the hair, and grinned at him. The pirate

spoke kindly to him, and tried to soothe him. 1808.
Lang, seeing himself deceived in his expectation,
and that he could not attain death by such
means, committed suicide,—being then a man
of seventy years of age.   Paou had really no intention to put Kwŏ lang to death, and he was
exceedingly sorry at what happened.   " We (8 v.)
others," said Paou, " are like vapours dispersed
by the wind ; we are like the waves of the sea,
roused up by a whirlwind ; like broken bamboo-
sticks on the sea, we are floating and sinking
alternately, without enjoying any rest.   Our
success in this fierce battle will, after a short
time, bring the united strength of government
on our neck.   If they pursue us in the different
windings and bays of the sea—they have maps
of them*.—should we not get plenty to do ? Who
will believe that it happened not by my command, and that I am innocent of the death of
this officer ?   Every man will charge me with
the wanton murder of a commander, after he had

* In the first preface of the Hae kwŏ hëen këen it is particularly stated, that the map of the sea-coast of China became first
known to its editor by the expeditions against the pirates.

1808. been vanquished and his ships taken? And they who have escaped will magnify my cruelty.* If I am charged with the murder of this officer, how could I venture, if I should wish in future times, to submit myself? Would I not be treated (9 r.) according to the supposed cruel death of Kwŏ lang?"

At the time that Kwŏ lang was fighting very bravely, about ten fisher-boats asked of the major Pang noo of the town Hëang shan,† to lend them the large guns, to assist the commander; but the major being afraid these fishermen might join the pirates,‡ refused their request.

* There are, as is stated in my preface, some vulgar or provincial characters in this history; here (p. 1.) occurs a character not to be found in Kanghe, composed out of the fifty-sixth radical and the group Leaou or Lew (7061, 7203). My whole library being locked up in the Custom-house, I am not able to consult a dictionary of the Canton dialect, therefore the meaning of these characters can only be guessed at by etymology. The etymology of the characters gives sometimes a better meaning than any dictionary, and sometimes it may entirely mislead us; there is no reliance on etymology. Usage is the only master of the Chinese, as of all other languages.

† Hëang shan is a considerable place between Macao and Canton. I passed this town in the beginning of October 1830. Distance from Canton 150 le in an eastern direction.

‡ It was, as we have before stated, the policy of Chang paou to befriend himself, when possible, with the lower sort of people.

And thus it happened, that the commander himself 1808. perished with many others. There were in the battle three of my friends : the lieutenant Tao tsae lin, Tseŏ tang hoo, and Ying tang hwang, serving under the former. Lin and Hoo were killed, but Hwang escaped when all was surrounded with smoke, and he it was who told me the whole affair.

On the eighth moon the general Lin fa went out as commander to make war against the pirates; but on seeing that they were so numerous, he became afraid, and all the other officers felt apprehensions ; he therefore tried to retire, but the pirates pursued after, and came up with him near a place called Olang pae.* The vessels (9 v.) in the front attacked the pirates, who were not able to move, for there happened to be a calm. But the pirates leaped into the water, and came swimming towards our vessels. Our commander

---

* Here the author himself says *Te ming* (9955, 7714) "name of a place." To find out the names of places and persons, and distinguish the titles of the different officers employed by government, is often a very difficult task. The last character in the name of this place, *pae*, is very seldom found ; it is the fourth character of the division of eight strokes, rad. 177.—See Kanghe. O is, in the Canton dialect, commonly pronounced like A, in Italian.

1808. not being able to prevent this by force, six vessels were taken ; and he himself, with ten other
men, were killed by the pirates.

A very large trading vessel called Teaou fa,
coming back laden with goods from Annam
and Tungking,* had a desperate skirmish with
the pirates. Chang paou, knowing very well
that he could not take her by force, captured
two ferry boats, and the pirates concealed themselves therein. Under the mask of ferrymen the
pirates pursued after, and called upon Teaou fa to
stop. Fa, confident in her strength, and that
victory would be on her side, let the ferrymen
come near, as if she had not been aware of the
(10 r.) deceit. But as soon as the pirates laid hold of
the ropes to board her, the trader's crew made a
vigorous resistance, and the pirates could not

* These are large vessels with windows, from 200 to 500 tons;
they are called by Europeans by the Chinese name, in the Canton
dialect, junks; *chuen* is the Mandarin pronunciation. The foreign
trade of Cochin-China and Tung king is almost exclusively with
China, that to Siam, Singapur, and Malacca, being inconsiderable.
The Cochin-Chinese government tried some years ago to open a
regular trade with Calcutta; but this undertaking partly failed on
account of the heavy duties on foreign sugar in the possessions of
the East-India Company. Sugar is a great article of export in
Cochin-China and Siam.

avail themselves of their knives and arrows— 1808.
guns they had not—the vessel being too large.
There were killed about ten hands in attacking
this vessel, and the pirates retired to their boat;
a circumstance which never happened before.

On the second moon of the fourteenth year, 1809.
the admiral *Tsuen mow sun* went on board his
flag vessel, called Mih teng, and proceeded with
about one hundred other vessels to attack the
pirates.   They were acquainted with his design
by their spies, and gathered together round
Wan shan;* the admiral following them in four
divisions.   The pirates, confident in their numbers, did not withdraw, but on the contrary
spread out their line, and made a strong attack.
Our commander looked very lightly on them, (10 v.)
yet a very fierce battle followed, in which many
were killed and wounded.   The ropes and sails
having been set on fire by the guns,† the pirates

---

* On the large map of the coast of China from Corea to Cochin-
China, called *Yuen* (12542) *hae tsuen too*, this place is called *Lao
wan shan*, "the old ten thousand mountains," and is exactly oppo
site to the Bocca Tigris in a direct southerly direction.

† The sails of Chinese vessels are often called Mats, for they are
really nothing else than matting,

1809. became exceeding afraid and took them away.
The commander directed his fire against the
steerage, that they might not be able to steer their
vessels. Being very close one to the other, the
pirates were exposed to the fire of all the four
lines at once. The pirates opened their eyes in
astonishment and fell down; our commander
advanced courageously, laid hold of their vessels,
killed an immense number of men, and took
about two hundred prisoners. There was a
pirate's wife in one of the boats, holding so fast
by the helm that she could scarcely be taken
away. Having two cutlasses, she desperately
defended herself, and wounded some soldiers;
but on being wounded by a musket-ball, she
(11 r.) fell back into the vessel and was taken prisoner.

About this time, when the red squadron was
assembled in Kwang chow wan, or the Bay of
Kwang chow, Tsuen mow sun went to attack
them; but he was not strong enough. The wife
of Ching yíh remained quiet; but she ordered
Chang paou to make an attack on the front of our
line with ten vessels, and Leang po paou to come
from behind. Our commander fought in the van

and in the rear, and made a dreadful slaughter; 1809.
but there came suddenly two other pirates, Hëang
shang url, and Suh puh king, who surrounded
and attacked our commander on all sides.   Our
squadron was scattered, thrown into disorder,
and consequently cut to pieces; there was a (11v.)
noise which rent the sky; every man fought in
his own defence, and scarcely a hundred remained together.   The squadron of Ching yïh
overpowered us by numbers; our commander
was not able to protect his lines, they were
broken, and we lost fourteen vessels.

Our men of war, escorting some merchant
vessels, in the fourth moon of the same year,
happened to meet the pirate nicknamed *The
Jewel of the whole crew*, cruizing at sea near a
place called Tang pae keŏ, outside of Tsëaou
mun.   The traders became exceedingly frightened, but our commander said: " This not
being the red flag, we are a match for them,
therefore we will attack and conquer them."
Then ensued a battle; they attacked each
other with guns and stones, and many people
were killed and wounded.   The fighting ceased

K

1809. towards the evening, and began again next
(12 r.) morning.   The pirates and the men of war
were very close to each other, and they boasted
mutually about their strength and valour.   It
was a very hard fight; the sound of cannon
and the cries of the combatants were heard
some le* distant.   The traders remained at some
distance; they saw the pirates mixing gunpowder in their beverage,—they looked instantly
red about the face and the eyes, and then
fought desperately.†   This fighting continued
three days and nights incessantly; at last becoming tired on both sides, they separated.

On the eighth day of the fifth moon the pirates
left their lurking place, attacked Kan chuh han,
and burned and plundered the houses.   On the
tenth they burned and plundered Kew këang,
(12v.) Sha kow, and the whole sea-coast; they then
turned about to Këe chow, went on shore, and
carried away fifty-three women by force.   They

---

* *Le :* this itinerary measure, as we have remarked, is different
in different parts of the empire; it is generally considered that 250
le make a degree of latitude.

† This they did probably to look more ferocious.   Plutarch ob-
serves of Sylla, that "the ferocity of his aspect was heightened
by his complexion, which was a strong *red*, interspersed with spots
of white."

went to sea again the following day, burned and 1809.
plundered on their way about one hundred houses
in Sin hwy and Shang sha, and took about a
hundred persons of both sexes prisoners.

On the sixth moon, the admiral Ting kwei
heu went to sea. Wishing to sail eastward, but
falling in with heavy rains for some days, he
stopped near Kwei këa mun,* and engaged in
settling concerning his ballast. On the eighth
day of this moon, Chang paou, availing himself
of the bad weather, explored the station in a
small boat and passed the place. Ting kwei was
right in thinking that the pirates would not undertake any thing during these heavy rains; but
he was careless regarding what might happen
after it. Indeed, as the weather cleared up on
the morning of the ninth, Chang paou appeared
suddenly before the admiral, and formed a line (13 r.)
of two hundred vessels. Ting kwei having no
sails ready, and all the ships being at anchor,
could by no means escape the pirates. The

---

* *Mun* means an *entrance* or *mouth*; few of these places are to
be found, even in the particular maps of the province Kwang tung
in the *Tay tsing hwy teen.*

1809. officers, being afraid of the large number of the
enemy, stood pale with apprehension near the
flagstaff, unwilling to fight. The admiral spoke
to them in a very firm manner, and said: "By
your fathers and mothers, by your wives and
children, do your duty; fight and destroy these
robbers. Every man must die: but should we
be so happy as to escape, our rewards from government will be immense. Should we fall in the
defence of our country, think that the whole force
of the empire will be roused, and they will try by
all means to destroy these banditti." They now
all united together in a furious attack, and sus-
(13v.) tained it for a long time: Ting kwei fired his
great guns,* and wounding the ringleader, nicknamed *The Jewel of the whole crew*, he fell down
dead.

The pirates were now at a loss how to proceed; but they received succour, while the force

* *Paou*, the first character of 8233, is in our own history always
used in the signification of *cannon*. The word meant in former
times an engine for throwing stones, and so it is used in the history
of the Han dynasty. This gave rise to the opinion that the Chinese had guns and gunpowder long before its discovery in Europe.
How could these extraordinary engines have escaped the discri-
minating genius of Marco Polo, had they existed in China?

of our commander diminished every moment. 1809.
About noon Paou drew nearer to the vessel of
Ting kwei, attacked her with small arms, and
sustained a great loss. But Leang po paou
suddenly boarded the vessel, and the crew was
thrown into disorder. Ting kwei seeing that
he was unable to withstand, committed suicide ;
while an immense number of his men perished
in the sea, and twenty-five vessels were lost.

Our former deputy-governor Pih ling was
about this time removed from his situation in
the three *Këang* to become governor-general of
the two Kwang.* People said, now that Pih (14 r.)
comes we shall not be overpowered by the
pirates. Old men crowded about the gates of
the public offices to make enquiries; the government officers appeared frightened and held
consultations day and night, and the soldiers
were ordered by a public placard to hold themselves ready to march. " Since the death of
Wang pëaou," it was said, " all commanders

* The three provinces which have Këang (5500) in their name,
the same as the two Kwang, Kwang to the east (tung) and Kwang
to the west (se), are usually united under one governor and one
deputy governor.

1809. were unfortunate.   Last year *Kwŏ lang lin* was killed in the battle at *Ma chow* ; *Tsuen mow sun* was unlucky at *Gaou kow*, *Url lin* ran away like a coward at *Lang pae*, and now *Ting kwei* has (14v.) again been routed at *Kwei kёa*.   If the valiant men let their spirits droop, and the soldiers themselves become frightened at these repeated defeats, the pirates will certainly overpower us at last; we can really not look for any assistance to destroy them.   We must try to cut off all provisions, and starve them."   In consequence of this, all vessels were ordered to remain, or to return into harbour, that the pirates might not have any opportunity to plunder, and thus be destroyed by famine.   The government officers being very vigilant about this regulation, the pirates were not able to get provisions for some months; they became at last tired of it, and resolved to go into the river itself.*

The pirates came now into the river by three different passages.†   The wife of Ching yĭh plundered about Sin hwy, Chang paou about

---

* Previously they robbed only in the open sea, outside the Canton river.

† The river discharges itself by many channels into the sea.

Tung kwan,* and O po tae about Fan yu † and 1809.
Shun tih, and all other smaller places con- (15 r.)
nected with Shun tih ; they were together explored by the pirates, who guarded the passage
from Fan to Shun.

On the first day of the seventh moon, O po tae
came with about a hundred vessels and burnt
the custom-house of Tsze ne. On the second day
he divided his squadron into four divisions, extending to Peih këang, Wei yung, Lin yo, Shïh
peih, and other villages. The *Chang lung* division ‡ surrounded the whole country from Ta
wang yin to Shwy sse ying. The *Ta chow*, or
large-vessel division, blockaded Ke kung shïh,
which is below the custom-house of Tsze ne.

---

* *Tung kwan hëen* is easterly from Canton 150 le, its area
amounts to 180 le, and pays 44,607 leang land-rent, or taxes.
There are many small islands belonging to the district of Tung
kwan.

† *Fan yu hëen*, near Canton. The place where European ships
anchor belongs to this Hëen ; its area amounts to 140 le, and pays
48,356 leang. I looked in vain for some notices regarding the
many small villages which are to be found in the sequel of the
page. Some of them are merely mentioned in the Itinerary of
the province Canton. The reader may compare the account of
Richard Glasspoole in the Appendix.

‡ These are names of different sorts of Chinese vessels or
junks.

1809. The pirates sent to the village Tsze ne, demand-
        ing ten thousand pieces of money * as tribute;
        and of San shen, a small village near Tsze ne
        on the right side, they demanded two thou-
(15 v.) sand.   The villagers differed in opinion; one
        portion would have granted the tribute, another
        would not.   That part who wished to pay the
        tribute said : " The pirates are very strong; it
        is better to submit ourselves now, and to give
        the tribute that we may get rid of them for
        awhile ; we may then with leisure think on
        means of averting any misfortunes which may
        befall us.   Our villages are near the coast, we
        shall be surrounded and compelled to do what
        they like, for no passage is open by which
        we can retire.   How can we, under such
        circumstances, be confident and rely on our own
        strength ?"

        The other part, who would not grant the tri-
        bute, said : " The pirates will never be satis-

        * In the original Kin (6369). Kin cannot be the common cash
    (Tung pao) for then the sum would be too trifling—8 to
    900 are to be got in Canton for a Spanish dollar. If Kin were
    used for dollar, or tael, which is very probable, the sum is
    enormous. Richard Glasspoole states that the pirates demanded
    indeed ten thousand dollars!—See the Appendix.

fied ; if we give them the tribute now, we shall 1809.
not be able to pay it on another day. If they
should make extortions a second time, where
should we get money to comply with their
demands? Why should we not rather spend
the two thousand pieces of money to encourage
government officers and the people? If we (16 r.)
fight and happen to be victorious, our place
will be highly esteemed ; but if, what heaven
may prevent, we should be unlucky, we shall
be everywhere highly spoken of." The day
drew to its end, and they could not agree in
what they should determine on, when one villager
arose and said : " The banditti will repeatedly
visit us, and then it will be impossible to pay
the tribute; *we must fight.*"

As soon as it was resolved to resist the demands of the pirates, weapons were prepared,
and all able men, from sixteen years and upwards to sixty, were summoned to appear with
their arms near the palisades. They kept quiet
the whole of the second day, and proceeded not
to fighting; but the people were much disturbed,
and did not sleep the whole night. On the fol-

L

1809. lowing day they armed and posted themselves
(16v.) on the sea-coast. The pirates, seeing that the
villagers would not pay the tribute, became enraged, and made a severe attack during the
night; but they could not pass the ditch before
the village. On the morning of the fourth, O po
tae headed his men, forced the ditch, took the
provisions, and killed the cattle. The pirates
in great numbers went on shore; but the villagers made such a vigorous resistance that they
began to withdraw. O po tae therefore surrounded the village on both sides, and the pirates
took possession of the mountain in the rear ;
they then threw the frightened villagers into disorder, pursued them, and killed about eighty.
After this the pirates proceeded with their van
to the sea-shore, without encountering any resistance from the front. The villagers were
from the beginning very much alarmed for their
(17 r.) wives and daughters; they collected them in
the temple and shut it up. But the pirates
being victorious, opened the temple, and carried
the women by force all away on board ship.
One pirate set off with two very fine women;

a villager, on seeing this, pursued after and 1809.
killed him in a hidden place. He then took the
women and carried them safe through the water,
—this was a servant. A great number of the
pirates were killed and wounded, and the villagers lost about two thousand persons. What
a cruel misfortune! it is hard indeed only to
relate it.

On the third day of the moon the people of
Ta ma chow, hearing that the pirates were
coming near, ran away. The pirates plundered
all that was left behind, clothes, cattle, and provisions. On the sixth day they came so far as (17v.)
Ping chow and San shan. On the eighth they
retired to Shaou wan, made an attack upon it
on the ninth, but could not take it. On the
tenth they ascended the river with the tide,
went on shore, and burned Wei shih tun. On
the eleventh day they came to our village, but
retired again at night on command. On the
twelfth they attacked Hwang yung, and left it
again on the thirteenth. They retired on the
fourteenth, and stopped at Nan pae. On the
fifteenth they sailed out of the Bocca Ti-

1809. gris,* and on the twenty-sixth attacked the
ships which bring the tribute from Siam,† but
were not strong enough to capture them. On
the twenty-ninth they attacked the places Tung
(18 r.) hwan and Too shin, and killed nearly a thousand
men.

The pirates tried many stratagems and
frauds to get into the villages. One came as
a country gentleman to take charge of the go-

* *Hoo mun.* The following notice on the Chinese tiger is
taken from the geography of Mookden, and translated by Father
Amiot. Eloge de la ville de Moukden par Kien long, p. 249.
" Au-delà de nos frontières (Mookden), il y a une espèce de tigre,
dont la peau est un fort beau blanc, sur lequel il y a, par intervalles,
des taches noires. Ces espèces de tigres sont plus méchants et
plus féroces que les autres." Father Amoit adds, that these tigers
are called *Hoo* by the Chinese, and *Tasha* by the Manchow.

† The Chinese geographers and historians are very well ac-
quaited with Siam; there is an interesting description of this empire in the Hae kwo hëen këen, p. 21, and in the 57th book, p. 13, of
the memoirs concerning the south of the Mei ling mountains. That
Siam acknowledges the supremacy of China, was known to the
most early European travellers. Cluver says (in his Introductio
in omnem Geographiam Wolfenbuttelæ, 1694, 4to., p. 473), that
" Rex Siamensis irruptione crebriori Tartarica pressus, Chano
denique Chinensi sese beneficiarium aut vasallum submisit."
Mendez Pinto, who was in that country in the year 1540, states
that the king of Siam acknowledged the supremacy of China;
Bernhardi Vareni Descriptio regni Japoniæ et Siam; Cantabrigiæ
1673-8, p. 128.

vernment guns; another came in a government 1809.
vessel as if to assist the village; after which
they on a sudden attacked and plundered all,
when people were not aware of them. One
pirate went round as a pedlar, to see and hear
all, and to explore every place. The country
people became therefore at last enraged, and
were in future always on their guard. If they
found any foreigner, they took him for a pirate
and killed him. So came once a government
officer on shore to buy rice ; but the inhabitants
thought he was a pirate and killed him. There
was every where a degree of confusion, which
it is impossible to explain.

On the sixteenth day of the seventh moon,
the pirates attacked a village near Tung kwan. (18v.)
The villagers knowing what would happen,
made fences and palisades, and obstructed the
passage with large guns. Armed with lances
and targets they hid themselves in a secret place,
and selected ten men only to oppose the pirates.
The pirates seeing that there were so few people,
went on shore to pursue them. As soon as
they came near the ambuscade the guns were

1809. fired ; the pirates became alarmed and dared not advance farther. Not being hurt by the fire, they again advanced; but three pirates presuming that there was an ambush, thought of retreating, and being very hard pressed by the enemy, they gave a sign to their comrades to come on shore. The ten villagers then retired near the ambush, and when the pirates pursued them, about a hundred were killed by their guns, and the whole force of the banditti was brought into disorder. The villagers pursued them kill-

(19 r.) ing many ; those also who had been taken alive were afterwards beheaded. They captured one small and two large vessels.*

On the eighteenth day of the eighth moon the wife of Ching yïh came with about five hundred vessels from Tung kwan and Sin hwy, and caused great commotion in the town Shun

---

* It is impossible to translate the names of vessels of different descriptions. The large are the Chang lung, or great dragon vessels which by the Chinese law are forbidden to be used by any private person; these are the Mandarin, or government vessels. The pirates nevertheless had such vessels, as likewise the daring smugglers, who bring the opium from Lintin, or Linting, to Canton. The amount of the opium trade in the port of Canton was, in the year 1829-30, equal to 12,057,157 Sp. dollars.

tih, Hëang shan, and the neighbouring places. 1809.
The squadron stopped at Tan chow, and on the
twentieth Chang pao was ordered to attack
Shaou ting with three hundred vessels. He
carried away about four hundred people, both
male and female ; he came also to the palisades
of our village, but could not penetrate inside.
The twenty-first he came to Lin tow, and the
twenty-second to Kan shin ; he made an attack, but could not overpower the place ; he
then returned to Pwan pëen jow, and lay before
its fence.   The inhabitants of Chow po chin, (19v.)
knowing that the pirates would make an attack,
assembled behind the wall to oppose them.
The pirates fired their guns and wounded some,
when the villagers ran away.   The pirates
then went on shore, but the villagers crowded
together and fired on them ; the pirates cast
themselves on the ground, and the shots passed
over their heads without doing any harm. Before the gunners could again load, the pirates
sprang up and put them to death.   Out of the
three thousand men who were in the battle,
five hundred were carried away by the pirates.

1809. One of the most daring pirates, bearing the
flag, was killed by the musket of a villager; a
second pirate then took the flag, and he also
was killed. The pirates now pressed against
the wall and advanced. There was also a fo-
(20 r.) reign pirate* engaged in the battle with a
fowling-piece. The pirates assembled in great
numbers to cut the wall with their halberts, but
they were disappointed on seeing they could
not attain their object in such a manner. The
pirates lost their hold, fell down, and were killed.
The engagement now became general, and great
numbers were killed and wounded on both
sides. The villagers at last were driven from
their fortifications, and the pirates pursued them
to *Mih ke*, or *the rocks about Mih,* where they
were hindered from going farther by foggy
weather; they retired and burned about twenty
houses, with all they contained. On the following day the pirates appeared again on the

---

* One of the English sailors, who had been taken prisoner.
" The pirates frequently obliged my men to go on shore and fight
with the muskets, which did great execution; the Chinese principally using bows and arrows. They have match-locks, but use
them very unskilfully."—See Appendix.

shore, but the inhabitants made a vigorous resis- 1809.
tance, and being driven back, they retired to
the citadel *Chih hwa*, where a thousand of them
fought so hard that the pirates withdrew. It (20 v.)
was reported that ten of them were killed, and
that the villagers lost eight men. On the twenty-
third the wife of Ching yïh ordered O po tae to
go up the river with about eighty vessels : he
stopped at Show ke and Kung shih. On the
twenty-fourth Chang paou and Po tae divided
this district between themselves, and robbed
and burned all. Pao had to plunder the north
part to Fo shin ; he carried away about ten
thousand stones of rice,* and burned down about
thirty houses ; on the twenty-fifth he went to Se
shin. O po tae came and burnt San heung keih ;
he then plundered Hwang yung, and came to
Këen ke, but did not make an attack against it.
He afterwards returned and laid waste Cha
yung.

* A shih, or stone, contains four keun : a keun thirty kin or
catty, the well known Chinese weight : a catty is equal to one
pound and a third English.

M

1809.   On the twenty-sixth Chang paou went up the
(21 r.) river to Nan hae* and Lan shïh. In the harbour
of the place were six rice vessels; and as soon
as Paou was in Lan shïh he made preparations
to capture these vessels. The military officer,
seeing that the pirates were numerous, remained however on his station, for the instant he
would have moved, Paou would have attacked
and captured him. Paou proceeded then against
the village itself; but the officer Ho shaou yuen
headed the inhabitants, and made some resistance. The pirates, nevertheless, mounted the
banks; and the villagers seeing their strength,
did not stay to fight—they became frightened
and ran away : all the others ran away without
making any resistance : Ho shaou yuen alone
opposed the banditti with a handful of people;
but he at last fell fighting, and the pirates burnt
(21 v.) four hundred shops and houses, and killed

* *Nan hae hïen.* Its area amounts to 278 le, and it pays 63,731
leang. The European factories in Canton lie in this district,
and the monastery opposite to the factories is usually from the
name of the district called the *Hae nan sze,* the temple of Hae
nan. The district of every place is called by the name of the
the place, and we must therefore speak of the town and district
Nan hae.

about ten persons. After the pirates had re- 1809.
tired, the inhabitants held in high esteem the
excellent behaviour of Ho shaou yuen ; they
erected him a temple, and the deputy-governor
Han fung performed sacrifices to his memory.

Shaou yuen was commanding officer in the
citadel of Lan shih ; he was of an active spirit,
and erected strong fences. Before the pirates
arrived, this was his daily discourse when he
spoke to the people : " *I know that I shall be
glorified this year by my death.*" Half the year
being already passed, it could not be seen how
this prophecy was to be fulfilled. When the
pirates came, he encouraged the citizens to oppose them vigorously ; he himself girded on
his sword and brandished his spear, and was
the most forward in the battle. He killed many
persons ; but his strength failed him at last,
and he was himself killed by the pirates. The
villagers were greatly moved by his excellent
behaviour; they erected him a temple, and said
prayers before his effigy. It was then known
what he meant, that " he would be glorified in
the course of the year." Now that. twenty

1809. years are passed, they even honour him by exhibiting fire-works. I thought it proper to subjoin this remark to my history.*

On the twenty-seventh, Lin sun mustered about forty vessels, and went out to fight with the pirates in order to protect the water passage. He remained at Kin kang (which is near

---

* This simple note of the Chinese author better illustrates the religion of China than many learned dissertations. All the deities, those of Greece and Rome, of China and India, are derived from two sources; both the powers of nature and highly gifted human beings were deified. These powers of nature, and the virtues and vices of men being in every community nearly similar, the same gods and goddesses are found every where; only their external form and shape is different. Every province, every town, and every village of China has its particular tutulary saint, or god, and on the day of his festival his effigy is carried in public. There is no essential difference in this respect between China and those countries where Roman Catholicism is yet in its highest vigour. The effigies of the Chinese gods and goddesses are all of the human shape; they have no monsters like India and Egypt, under which it was once the fashion to seek for extraordinary wisdom and astonishing science. Lucian has already taken the liberty of laughing at these deities, and at the writers, the prophets, and sophists, who try to find some sense in all this vulgar display of nonsense, by which the people are deluded. Lucian de Sacreficiis s. f. where he laughs at the Jupiter with a ram's head, at the good fellow Mercurius with the countenance of a dog, etc. Κριοπρόσωπον μὲν τὸν Δία, κυνοπρόσωπον δὲ τὸν βέλτιστον Ἑρμῆν καὶ τὸν Πᾶνα ὅλον τραγὸν, etc. See the pleasant story of Jupiter with the ram's head in Herodotus, II. 42.

Shaou wan hae), hid himself westerly of that 1809.
place the whole day, and removed then to Tsze (22 r.)
ne. Chang paou ordered his vessels to remove to
Shaou ting, and his men to go on shore in the
night-time. Sun, seeing with sorrow that the
pirates were so numerous, and that he could
not make any effectual resistance, ran away
eastwards and hid himself at Peih keang. At
daylight the following morning the pirates
sailed to Tsze ne to attack our commander, but
not finding him, they stopped at Shaou ting;
for this being the time when the autumnal winds
begin to blow, they were afraid of them, and made
preparations to retire. But we shall soon find
the different flags returning to the high sea to
fight both with extraordinary courage and great
ferocity.*

On the twenty-ninth they returned to plunder (22 v.)
Kan shin; they went into the river with small
vessels, and the inhabitants opposing them,
wounded two pirates, which all the pirates re-
sented. They next came with large vessels, sur-

* The strong winds (Tay fung) in the Chinese sea begin about
the middle of September, or just before the equinox.

1809. rounded the village, and made preparations to
(22v.) mount the narrow passes. The inhabitants re-
       mained within the intrenchments, and dared
       not come forward. The pirates then divided
       their force according to the various passes, and
       made an attack. The inhabitants prepared
       themselves to make a strong resistance near the
       entrance from the sea on the east side of the
       fence; but the pirates stormed the fence, planted
       their flag on the shore, and then the whole
       squadron followed. The inhabitants fought
       bravely, and made a dreadful slaughter when
       the pirates crossed the entrance at Lin tow.
       The boxing-master, Wei tang chow, made a vi-
       gorous resistance, and killed about ten pirates.
       The pirates then began to withdraw, but Chang
       paou himself headed the battle, which lasted
       very long. The inhabitants were not strong
       enough. Wei tang was surrounded by the pirates;
(23r.) nevertheless that his wife fought valiantly by
       his side. On seeing that they were surrounded
       and exhausted, the father of the lady* rushed

       * It is not stated in the Chinese text, whose father rushed for-
       ward, whether it was the father of the lady, or of Wei tang chow.

forward and killed some pirates. The pirates 1809. then retired in opposite directions, in order to surround their opponents in such a manner that they might not escape, and could be killed without being able to make any resistance ; and thus it happened, the wife of Wei tang being slain with the others.

The pirates now pursued the inhabitants of the place, who cut the bridge and retired to the neighbouring hills. The pirates swam through the water and attacked the inhabitants, who were unable to escape. The whole force of the pirates being now on shore, the inhabitants suffered a severe loss,—it is supposed about a hundred of them were killed; the loss of the pirates also was considerable. (23 v.)

The pirates went in four divisions to plunder; they took here an immense quantity of clothes and other goods, and carried away one thousand one hundred and forty captives of both sexes. They set on fire about ten houses; the flames could not be extinguished for some days; in the whole village you could not hear

1809. the cry of a dog or a hen. The other inhabitants retired far from the village, or hid
themselves in the fields. In the paddy fields
about a hundred women were hidden, but the
pirates on hearing a child crying, went to the
place and carried them away. *Mei ying*, the
wife of Ke choo yang, was very beautiful, and a
(24 r.) pirate being about to seize her by the head, she
abused him exceedingly. The pirate bound her
to the yard-arm ; but on abusing him yet more,
the pirate dragged her down and broke two of
her teeth, which filled her mouth and jaws with
blood. The pirate sprang up again to bind her.
Ying allowed him to approach, but as soon as he
came near her, she laid hold of his garments with
her bleeding mouth, and threw both him and
herself into the river, where they were drowned.
The remaining captives of both sexes were after
some months liberated, on having paid a ransom
of fifteen thousand leang or ounces of silver.

Travelling once to Pwan pëen jow I was
affected by the virtuous behaviour of *Mei ying*,
and all generous men will, as I suppose, be

moved by the same feelings. I therefore com- 1809.
posed a song, mourning her fate :

    Chén ké kīn seāou hëĕ,
    Chúy szē chūng soó mëèn.
    Tāng shē shwŭy fàn leïh,
    Yēw nèu tŭh nāng tsūy ;
    Tsëĕn hēuĕ yīng kwáng nëĕ,*
    Yuēn keŭ yuēn shwŭy weī.
    Shwūy hwăn pō shàng heà,
    Yīng lëĕ sháng pèi hwūy.

Cease fighting now for awhile!
Let us call back the flowing waves!
Who opposed the enemy in time ?
A single wife could overpower him.
Streaming with blood, she grasped the mad offspring (24 v.)
    of guilt,
She held fast the man and threw him into the mean-
    dering stream.
The spirit of the water, wandering up and down on
    the waves,
Was astonished at the virtue of *Ying.*
    My song is at an end !
Waves meet each other continually.

* I must again remark that there is a false character in our
text: it should be Nëĕ, 7974 in the Tonical Dictionary of
Dr. M.

N

1809.   I see the water green as mountain Peih,

But the brilliant fire returns no more !*

How long did we mourn and cry !†

* I am compelled to give a free translation of this verse, and
confess myself not quite certain of the signification of the
poetical figures used by our author. *Fŭng* signifies a hollow
pyramid filled with combustibles; *yĕn* signifies the smoke caused
by combustion; *tseāng* signifies the spar or yard in a boat or ship,
to which the sail is attached, and *ying* is shadow. It seems that
the author alludes to the spar or yard-arm, at which *Mei ying* was
fastened by the pirate; but what he means by *shadow* I do not
really know, perhaps *ying* is in the place of *Mei ying*.

† The Chinese characters are printed like the other portion of
the work. I have divided them according to the verses. Only the
first eight lines have a regular metre of five feet, or words, and as
the author himself says, his song is then at an end; but the language still remains poetical, and for that reason it was thought
proper to divide also the remaining lines like verses. Every word
must be considered as consisting of one syllable or sound, even if
we write it with three or four vowels. Poetry is perhaps more
esteemed in China, than in any other country in the world. The
late governor-general of Kwang tung and Kwang se, his Excellency Yuen, published the poems of his daughter, who died
when only nineteen years of age. Most of the emperors of
China wrote verses, and I have, if I remember rightly, an imperial collection printed at the command of Kĕa king of many
volumes, containing the poetry of the crowned heads of China.
The reader may easily imagine that the Chinese have many works
on poetry; I am also in possession of a Chinese *Gradus ad Par-
nassum* in ten large volumes, in which are to be found, divided under
different heads, all the fine expression and poetical images of the
classical poets. Mr. Davis has given some excellent specimens
of Chinese poetry in his elegant dissertation on that subject.

BOOK SECOND.

———◆———

ON the thirteenth day of the ninth moon our 1809.
Admiral Tsuen mow sun mustered about eighty (1 r.)
vessels to go to Shaou wan, and obstruct the
passage. The pirates heard of these preparations, and on the night of the fourteenth every
vessel of the different flags was ordered to go
to Shaou wan. Their order was, that being
within ten le from the place, they should stop
and prepare themselves to begin the battle
when it was dark. From the first night watch
the cannon began to fire, and only ceased with (1 v.)
daylight. At the end of the day the cannon
were again roaring without any intermission, and
the country people mounted on the green Lo
shang, to look at the progress of the fight.
They saw the wrecks of vessels floating on the
sea, the waves were rolling, the bullets flying,

1809. and the cries of dying people mounted to the skies. The vallies re-echoed the noise; beasts and birds* started alarmed, and found no place where they might repose themselves. The vessels were thrown into disorder, and our army was pressed down by the overpowering force of the enemy. Our commander lost four vessels, but the palisade before the village could not be taken, by which means it was protected against pillage. Our admiral said, " Since I cannot conquer these wicked pirates, I will blow myself up." In this manner the
(2 r.) admiral and many other officers met their death.

On the twenty-fifth the pirates went to Hëang shan and to great Hwang po ;† they took pos-

---

* Verbally " monkeys and birds," a sort of birds which according to Dr. Morrison are something similar to our crows.

† In the memoirs concerning the south of the Meiling mountains, three books (from 9—11 incl.) are filled up with a description of the seas, rivers, and lakes, of the province of Canton. Book ninth begins with a general description of the Chinese seas, and of the different entrances from the sea-side ; then follows a particular description of the sea near Canton and Hainan, and of the different Tides at various places. The mariner would certainly be gratified by a translation of this part of the work. The translator has often remarked the extraordinary phenomenon of the fiery appearance of the sea, during his residence in China.

session of the inside and the outside passage of 1809. Hwang po, so that the boat-people,* who stay

---

In the before-mentioned work, b. ix. p. 5 v, we read the following notice concerning this phenomenon :

" *The fire in the sea :* It happens sometimes that sea waves have such a luminous appearance, as if the whole sea were full of fire. If you cast any thing into the sea, it becomes luminous like a star ; but you do not see this during moonlight. Wood having in itself no fire, receives a fiery appearance, after having been passed through the water."

In b. x. p. 10 r. Whampo is said to be seventy le from the sea custom-house of Canton. In this extract foreigners are in general very unfavourably spoken of. Amongst other things we are told, " that foreigners or barbarians drink so much strong liquor that they are not able to stand on their feet; they fall down intoxicated, and before having had a sound sleep, they cannot rise again." It is also remarked in the same article that many people assemble together at Whampo, to attend the trade with the foreigners ; the reason probably why our author calls it " the Great." The reader will remember what has been said on Hëang shan in a former note ; I will only here add the remark of Martini, " that in his time the principal and most wealthy merchants lived in that place." (Thevenot Rélations de divers voyages, iii. 167.)

* It is well known that a great part of the population of China live on the water, and they are generally called *Tan* (9832) people;—a word which in the Canton dialect is pronounced *Tanka*. They are quite a separate race, and harshly dealt with by the Chinese government. There exist particular works concerning the history, the customs and laws of these boat-people. They more than once opposed the despotic regulation of their masters, and government was always afraid they might join the pirates. The history of the southern barbarians in the often

1809. outside on the coast, retired and came up to
the town with their boats.   The military officer
Ting gaou ho being made acquainted with the
arrival of the pirates, requested ten fishing
boats from the town Hëang shan to assist the
citizens and to help them in opposing the
enemy.   He posted himself before the town to
protect it.   Ting gaou behaved valiantly on the
river ; he headed his small fleet of fishing boats
and opposed the pirates.   There was incessant
(2 v.) fighting day and night ; but at last the numerous vessels of the pirates surrounded him on
all sides, and Ting gaou ho received a severe
wound in the back.   He then addressed his
comrades in the following words : " Being on

---

quoted *Memoirs*, &c. begins with a description of the *Tan jin*, or
Tanka people, and it is there said that they are divided into three
different classes. The description of their customs and manners
is very interesting, and I hope soon to lay it before the English
reader. It has been supposed that the name *Tanka people* is derived from the form of their boats, which is similar to an *egg* ;
but *Shwŏ wăn*, as quoted in Kang he, explains the word only by
Nan fang c yay, Barbarians of the southern region.   There exist
different forms of this character, but I think we should not
presume to make an etymology of a Chinese character without
being authorized by the Shwŏ wăn, the oldest and most genuine
source of Chinese lexicography.

the military station before this town, it was my 1802.
intention to destroy the pirates, and for this
reason I united with all the principal men to
oppose them, without considering my own
safety ;—joyful I went to oppose the enemy.
But not being able to destroy this immense number of banditti, I am now surrounded with all
my principal men ; and being deficient in
power, I will die.   Death could not move me,
but I fear the cruel behaviour of the banditti ;
I fear that if the battle come to its highest
summit, our fathers and mothers, our wives and
sons, will be taken captives.   United with the
principal men of the town, we cannot destroy
the pirates, neither protect the country, our (3 r.)
families, nor our own firesides,—but the circumstances being desperate, we must do our
utmost.*

   They now again rushed against the pirates
and killed many of them ; but their strength

   * In the Chinese text is *King king* (the character is composed
out of radical *fire* and *ear*), on which is to be found an interesting
critical observation in Kang he, s. v. b. viii. p. 119r.   In no other
oriental language has there been so much done by the natives for
the foreign student as by the Chinese.

1809. being exhausted, the ten fishing boats were
taken, and great Hwang po given up to be plundered. The citizens retired to their intrenchments, and made such vigorous resistance that
the pirates could not make them captives.
Chang paou therefore ordered O po tae and Leang
po paou to make an attack on both sides, on the
front and the rear at once; so the citizens sustained a great defeat, and about a hundred of
them were killed. A placard was then posted
up in the town, admonishing the citizens that
they being unable to resist the enemy, must,
under these cruel circumstances, send mes-
sengers to make terms with the pirates. This
(3 v.) being done, the pirates withdrew.

The wife of Ching yih then ordered the pirates
to go up the river; she herself remaining with
the larger vessels in the sea to blockade the
different harbours or entrances from the sea-
side; but the government officers made preparations to oppose her. There were about this
time three foreign vessels returning to Portugal.*

---

* The most common denomination for Portugal is now Se
yang kwŏ, or more correctly *Siao se yang kwŏ.* " The small

Yïh's wife attacked them, took one vessel, and 1809.
killed about ten of the foreigners; the two
other vessels escaped.   The Major Pang noo of
Hëang shan about this time fitted out a hundred
vessels to attack the pirates; he had before
hired six foreign vessels, and the two Portuguese
ships, which had before run away, united also
with him.   Yïh's wife, seeing that she had not
vessels enough, and that she might be surrounded, ordered a greater number to her assistance. (4 r.)
She appointed Chang paou to command them,
and sail up the river; but to keep quiet with
his squadron till he saw the Chang lung, or
government vessels come on.   On the third of
the tenth moon the government vessels went
higher up the river, and Chang paou following
and attacking them, the foreign vessels sustained a great loss, and all the other vessels

realm in the western ocean; Europe is called *Ta se yang.* (See
Preface.) I thought it here more proper to translate *E* by *foreigner*,
than by *barbarian*. In a Chinese history of Macao, we find various
particulars regarding the Portuguese. The description of the
Portuguese clergy and the Roman Catholic religion is the most interesting part of this curious publication. It consists of two parts,
or volumes.

1809. then ran away. The foreigners showed themselves very courageous; they petitioned the
mayor of Hëang shan to place himself at the
head of the foreign vessels, to go and fight the
pirates. Pang noo having for some time considered their request, inspected on the tenth of
the same month the six foreign vessels, their
arms and provisions, and went out into the sea
(4v.) to pursue the pirates.

About this time Chang paou had collected his
force at Ta yu shan near Chih leih keŏ, and the
foreign vessels went thither to attack him.
About the same time the admiral, Tsuen mow
sun, collected a hundred vessels, and joined the
foreigners to attack the pirates. On the thirteenth they spread out their lines, and fought
during two days and two nights, without either
party proving victorious. On the fifteenth one
of the officers went forward with some large
vessels to attack the pirates, but he was very
much hurt by the fire of the guns; his vessel
was lost, and about ten men were killed and
many others wounded,—after this, the whole
fleet retired. They however again commenced

fighting on the sixteenth, but being unable to 1809.
withstand the pirates, one vessel more was
lost.*

The Admiral Tsuen mow sun was exceed- (5 r.)
ingly eager to destroy the pirates, but he was
confident that he was not strong enough to vanquish them, and he spoke thus to his people :
" The pirates are too powerful, we cannot master
them by our arms; the pirates are many, we
only few; the pirates have large vessels, we only
small ones ; the pirates are united under one
head, but we are divided,—and we alone are
unable to engage with this overpowering force.
We must therefore now make an attack, when
they cannot avail themselves of their number,
and contrive something besides physical strength,
for by this alone it is impossible for us to be victorious.   The pirates are now all assembled in
Ta yu shan, a place which is surrounded by
water. Relying on their strength, and thinking (5 v.)

---

* It would be interesting to read the Portuguese version of
these skirmishes. A history of these skirmishes was printed at
Lisbon, but I could not procure this publication. The reader may
compare the statements of Richard Glasspoole in the Appendix.

1809. that they will be able to vanquish us, they will
certainly not leave this place of retirement. We
should therefore from the provincial city (Canton)
assemble arms and soldiers as many as we can,
surround the place, and send fire-vessels among
their fleet. It is probable that in such a manner
we may be able to measure our strength with
them."

In consequence of this determination all
commanders and officers of the different vessels
were ordered to meet on the seventeenth at Chih
leih keŏ, to blockade the pirates in Ta yu shan,
and to cut off all supplies of provisions that
might be sent to them. To annoy them yet
more, the officers were ordered to prepare the
materials for the fire-vessels. These fire-vessels
were filled with gunpowder, nitre, and other
combustibles ; after being filled, they were set on
(6 r.) fire by a match from the stern, and were instantly
all in a blaze. The Major of Hëang shan, Pang
noo, asked permission to bring soldiers with him,
in order that they might go on shore and make
an attack under the sound of martial music,
during the time the mariners made their pre-

paration. On the twentieth it began to blow very 1809.
fresh from the north, and the commander ordered
twenty fire-vessels to be sent off, when they took,
driven by the wind, an easterly direction; but
the pirate's entrenchments being protected by a
mountain, the wind ceased, and they could not
move farther on in that direction; they turned
about and set on fire two men of war. The
pirates knowing our design were well prepared
for it; they had bars with very long pincers, by
which they took hold of the fire-vessels and kept
them off, so that they could not come near.
Our commander, however, would not leave the
place; and being very eager to fight, he ordered (6 v.)
that an attack should be made, and it is presumed that about three hundred pirates were
killed. Pao now began to be afraid, and asked
the *Spirit of the three Po*, or old mothers, to give
a prognostic. The *Pŭh*, or lot for fighting, was
disastrous; the *Pŭh*, or lot to remain in the
easterly entrenchment, was to be happy. The
Pŭh, or lot for knowing if he might force the
blockade or not on leaving his station to-mor-

1809. row, was also happy,* three times one after
another.

There arose with the day-light on the twenty-
second a light southerly breeze; all the squadrons began to move, and the pirates prepared
themselves joyfully to leave their station.
About noon † there was a strong southerly
wind, and a very rough sea on. As soon as it
became dark the pirates made sail, with a good
deal of noise, and broke through the blockade,

* The Chinese are very much accustomed to consult the Pŭh,
or sort. There exists various ways, according to the ideas of the
Chinese, of asking the divinity whether any undertaking shall
prove either fortunate or not. The translator has seen different
modes of casting lots in the temples of the suburbs of Canton.
The reader may find an interesting description of casting lots in
the "Histoire du grand Royaume de la Chine;" à Rouen 1614-8,
p. 30. There is much useful information to be found in this
work; but it would be curious to learn in what Armenian works
("escritures des Armeniens") it is stated, that "St. Thomas came
through China in his voyage to the East-Indies" (l. c. p. 25)!

† _Woo_ (11753) _how; Woo_ is the time between eleven and one
o'clock of the day. The Chinese divide the day into twelve _she
shin_, or great hours; the European twenty-four hours of the day
are called _seaou she shin_, little hours. We learn by a passage of
Herodotus (Euterpe 109), that the Greeks in his time also divided
the day into twelve parts; Herodotus also adds that the Greeks received this division of time from the Babylonians.—See Visdelou
in the Supplement to the "Bibliothèque Orientale," by Herbelot,
under the word _Fenek_.

favoured by the southerly wind. About a hun- 1809.
dred vessels were upset, when the pirates left
Ta yu shan. But our commander being un-
aware that the pirates would leave their entrenchments, was not prepared to withstand
them. The foreign vessels fired their guns and (7 r.)
surrounded about ten leaky vessels, but could
not hurt the pirates themselves; the pirates left
the leaky vessels behind and ran away. After
this they assembled outside at Hung chow in
the ocean.

Notwithstanding that the pirates had broken
through the blockade, Tsuen mow sun desisted
not from pursuing them; he followed the pirates
into the open sea in order to attack them. On
the fifth of the eleventh moon he met the pirates
near Nan gaou, and prepared his vessels* to
attack them. The pirates spread out all their
vessels one by one, so that the line of their fleet
reached the forces of our commander; they then
tried to form a circle and surround our admiral.
Our commander, in order to prevent this, divided
his force,—he separated from him eighty vessels, (7 v.)

* *Me teny* is a particular sort of junk.

1809. which had orders to join him afterwards. Before they united again, a great battle took place
between the two fleets; the firing lasted from
three till five in the afternoon; our crew fought
exceedingly hard and burnt three pirate-vessels.
The pirates retreated, and our navy declined
pursuing them, because it would carry them
too far out of the way. Our crew being still
elated at this transaction, the pirates on a
sudden returned, roused them out of their sleep
and constrained them to fight a second time.
The commander had no time to make preparations, so that two vessels were burnt by the
fire of the pirates, and three were captured.

(8 r.)   At the time when Chang paou was blockaded
in Chih leih keŏ, and was afraid that he should
not be able to come out again, he sent to O po
tae, who was at Wei chow, to rescue him. His
message was in the following words :—" I am
harassed by the government's officers outside in
the sea; lips and teeth must help one another,
if the lips are cut away the teeth will feel cold.
How shall I alone be able to fight the government
forces ? You should therefore come at the head

of your crew, to attack the government squadron 1809,
in the rear, I will then come out of my station
and make an attack in front ; the enemy being
so taken in the front and rear, will, even supposing we cannot master him, certainly be
thrown into disorder."

Ever since the time Paou was made chieftain
there had been altercations between him and O
po tae. Had it not have been out of respect for
the wife of Ching yïh they would perhaps have (8 v.)
made war against each other. Till now they
only showed their mutual dislike in their plundering expeditions on the ocean, and in consequence of this jealousy Po tae did not fulfil the
orders of Paou. Paou and his whole crew felt
very much annoyed at this conduct, and having
been able to break through the blockade, he
resolved to measure his strength with Tae. He
met him at Neaou chow, and asked him : " Why
did you not come to my assistance ?"

O po tae answered : " You must first consider
your strength and then act ; you must consider
the business and then go to work. How could
I and my crew have been sufficient against the

P

1809. forces of the admiral. I learnt your request, but men being dependent upon circumstances, I could not fulfil it; I learnt your request, but I was dependent on circumstances, and men (9 r.) cannot act otherwise.* And now concerning this business—to give or not give assistance— am I bound to come and join your forces?"

Paou became enraged and said: " How is this, will you then separate from us?"

Tae answered : " I will not separate myself."

Paou : " Why then do you not obey the orders of the wife of Ching yïh and my own? What is this else than separation, that you do not come to assist me, when I am surrounded by the enemy? I have sworn it that I will destroy thee, wicked man, that I may do away with this soreness on my back."

There passed many other angry words between them, till they at length prepared to fight and destroy each other. Chang paou was the first to begin the battle; but having fired his

---

† These speeches seem to be rhetorical exercises of the Chinese historian; the antithesis is a figure very much used in Chinese rhetoric and poetry, and a great part of their poetry consists merely of such antitheses.

guns, and being deficient in strength, Tae went 1809.
against him with all his well prepared forces.
Paou was not able to make any effectual resistance to his enemy ; he received a severe defeat,
he lost sixteen vessels, and three hundred men (9 v.)
were taken prisoners. The prisoners were all
killed from mutual hatred.

O po tae remained then at the head of his
forces without any opposition, since Paou withdrew. There was now a meeting held under
these banditti ; when Chang jih kao arose and
said :

" If Paou and we should again measure our
strength against each other, our force will not be
found sufficient; we are only one to ten. It is
to be feared that they will collect all their forces
together to exterminate us. They may on a
sudden come against us and make an attack,—
our small body must certainly be in fear of their
vast number. There is *Leang po paou*, an experienced pirate on the sea ; if he should on
a sudden turn his vessels against us, there is not
one among us who would be able to resist him.
He is a very zealous worshipper of the spirit of

1809. the three Po or Mothers, and protected by
       them; nay, and protected by them in a super-
(10 r.) natural manner.   But if we perform sacrifices,
       they remain without shadow and echo.*   And
       then it may also be added that we are no more
       able to withstand with our short arms their long
       ones, than dogs are able to chase fierce tigers.
       But do we not every where see government
       placards inviting us to submit, why do we not
       then send somebody to make the offer?   The
       government will pardon and not destroy us
       sea-monsters,† and we may then reform our
       previous conduct.   Why should we not therefore
       come to a determination to that effect?"

       Fung yung fa said: "How then if govern-
       ment should not trust our word?"

       Chang jih kao answered: "If government
       should learn that we recently fought Chang
(10 v.) paou, and destroyed the banditti,—it would

---

* That is—they are of no effect at all.   I, however, thought it
proper to retain the strong figure of the original.

† The author forgets in his rhetorical flourishes, that it is a
pirate himself who speaks to pirates.   The Chinese characters for
" sea monster" are to be found in M 2057; " *King e* is used figu-
ratively for a devouring conqueror of men," says Dr. Morrison.

be hard indeed if that were not enough to make 1809.
them trust us?"

Go tsew he said : " If government should not
act towards us, as it is stated in the placard,
after having made our submission, we may then
again use violence. But they will hear, that we
attacked the others, like fishes their food ; that
we alone made a beginning in destroying the
pirates, and then tendered our submission,—they
will feel that they can employ us to destroy
the other pirates. He who is not of the same
opinion as mine may let his hand hang down."

O po tae was of the same opinion, and the
purser was ordered to frame the offer of submission to government. The petition concerning
the offer was couched in the following terms :

" It is my humble opinion that all robbers of
an overpowering force, whether they had their
origin from this or any other cause, have felt the (11 r.)
humanity of government at different times.
Leang shan who three times plundered the city,
was nevertheless pardoned and at last made a
minister of state.* Wa kang often challenged

* The author has here the expression *tung-leang* (11399) *pillar*,
in its proper and figurative sense. He probably chose this ex-

1809. the arms of his country and was suffered to live, and at last made a corner-stone of the empire. Joo ming pardoned seven times Mang hwŏ; and Kwan kung three times set Tsaou tsaou at liberty.* Ma yuen pursued not the exhausted robbers; and Yŏ fei killed not those who made their submission. There are many other instances of such transactions both in former and recent times, by which the country was strength-

(11 v.) ened and government increased its power. We now live in a very populous age; some of us could not agree with their relations, and were driven out like noxious weeds. Some after having tried all they could, without being able to provide for themselves, at last joined bad society. Some lost their property by shipwrecks; some

pression to make, according to Chinese sentiments, a fine rhetorical phrase. *Leang* in the beginning of the phrase corresponds to the sound and the form of the character to *Leang* at the end: Leang shan san kĕĕ ching yĭh, mung găn shay url king tsŏ tung-leang. There is also something like a quibble in the second phrase; Wa kang, *Bricks and mountain ridge* is transformed into Choo shĭh (1223) or a *corner-stone*, just as Leang-shan, *mountain bridge* is into tung-leang, or a *pillar*.

* O po tae alludes to well known events in Chinese history. On Tsaou tsaou see Dr. Morrison, 10549 in the tonical part of the Dictionary.

withdrew into this watery empire to escape from 1809.
punishment. In such a way those, who in the
beginning were only three or five, were in the
course of time increased to a thousand or ten
thousand, and so it went on increasing every
year. Would it not have been wonderful if
such a multitude, being in want of their daily
bread, should not have resorted to plunder and
robbery to gain their subsistence, since they
could not in any other manner be saved from
famine? It was from necessity that the laws
of the empire were violated, and the merchants
robbed of their goods. Being deprived of our
land and of our native places, having no house
or home to resort to, and relying only on the (12 r.)
chances of wind and water, even could we for
a moment forget our griefs, we might fall in
with a man-of-war, who with stones, darts
and guns, would blow out our brains." " Even
if we dared to sail up a stream and boldly go
on with anxiety of mind under wind, rain, and
stormy weather, we must every where prepare
for fighting. Whether we went to the east, or to
the west, and after having felt all the hardships

1809. of the sea, the night dew was our only dwelling, and the rude wind our meal.   But now we will avoid these perils, leave our connexions, and desert our comrades; we will make our submission.   The power of government knows no bounds; it reaches to the islands in the sea, and every man is afraid and sighs.   Oh we must be destroyed by our crimes, none can escape who opposeth the laws of government. (12v.) May you then feel compassion for those who are deserving of death; may you sustain us by your humanity!"

The chief officers of government met joyfully together at Canton.   The governor-general of the southern district ever loved the people like himself; and to show his benevolence he often invited them by public placards to make submission:— he really felt compassion for these lower sort of men, who were polluted with crimes.   The way of compassion and benevolence is the way of heaven, which is pleased with virtue; it is the right way to govern by righteousness.   Can the bird remain quiet with strong wings, or will the fish not move in deep water?   Every person acts from natural endowments, and our general 1809. would have felt compassion even for the mean- est creature on earth, if they would have asked for pardon. He therefore redeemed these pirates from destruction, and pardoned their former crimes.*

After this period the country began to assume a new appearance. People sold their arms and (13 r.) bought oxen to plough their fields; they burned sacrifices, said prayers on the top of the hills, and rejoiced themselves by singing behind screens during day-time. There were some people who endeavoured to act with duplicity, and wished to murder the pirates, but the general on seeing the petition said to his assistants : " I will pull down the vanguard of the enemy to use it for the destruction of the remaining part. I may then employ it against the over-spreading power of the pirates ; with the pirates I will destroy the pirates. Yŏ fu mow destroyed in this manner

* I confess that it was not an easy matter to translate these rhetorical exercises and poetical phrases, by which the author is evidently anxious to draw a veil over the weakness of the empire. The Chinese scholar will certainly pardon any mistake which might occur in this poetical or furious prose—to use the expression of Blair in his *Lectures on Rhetoric.*

Q

1809. Yang tay : let us not act with duplicity, that we
may the better disperse their comrades and
break their power; let us therefore accept their
submission."

In the agreement it was stipulated that the
ships should assemble together in the open sea
near Kwei shen hëen* to make their surrender.
The Governor-general was to come to that place
(13v.) to receive O po tae, his vessels, his men, and
all other things which were pointed out in the
petition. The Governor-general being exceedingly pleased, ordered his adjutant Kung gaou
to examine the list. He found eight thousand
men, one hundred and twenty-six vessels, five
hundred large guns, and five thousand six hundred various military weapons. The towns Yang
keang and Sin gan were appointed for this
people to live in.†—This happened in the

* *Kwei shen* is a Hëen or town of the third rank, and dependent
on the district metropolis Hwy chow foo; it is near to Hwy. Its
area amounts to thirty-seven le, and pays in taxes 26,058 leang.
It is stated in the *Itinerary of Canton* (Kwang tung tsuen too,
p. 5. v.) that the situation of this great town makes it a place of
danger; being close to the sea, Kwei shen is exposed to sudden
attacks from pirates.

† *Yang keang* is a town of the third rank, and dependent on

twelfth month of the fourteenth year of Këa Jan.
king—and so the black squadron was brought $^{1810.}$
into subjection.   O po tae changed his name to
Heŏ bëen, " The lustre of instruction," and the
general made him a Pa tsung* to reward his
services in defeating Chang paou.

On the twelfth moon Chang paou went with (14 r.)
his different squadrons into the river and attacked Ke chow.   It was near the end of the year,
and the pirates assembled along the mountain

---

its district metropolis Chow king foo; distant from Chow king
foo in a southerly direction 340 le.   Its area amounts to twenty-
nine le, and it pays 12,499 leang in taxes.

Sin gan is a town of the third rank, and dependent upon
Kwang chow foo ; distance from Canton in a north-east direction
200 le.   Its area amounts to fifty le, and pays in taxes 11,623 leang.
There are three towns in the district of Canton, whose names
begin with *Sin*, new ; *Sin hwy*, *The New Association ; Sin ning*,
The New Repose ; and *Sin gan*, *The New Rest*.   Kwang tung tsuen
too p. 3 v. 4 v et r. 8 r, *Ning* (8026) is now always written without
sin or heart, being the *ming* or proper name of the reigning emperor.   By a mistake it is stated in the Indo-Chinese Gleaner
(iii. 108.), that *Ning* was the proper name of Këa king.   The
proper name of the reigning emperor is considered sacred, and
must be spelled differently during his life-time.

* A Pa tsung, a kind of inferior military officer, says Dr.
Morrison, under the word pa, (8103.)

1810. ridge Laou ya* to make a festival : they made a great noise during the night with crackers, and their gongs were heard at a great distance.†

At daybreak the flags were spread out, and the drums sounded ; they were cheerful the whole day ; they eat and drank and made a great noise, which was heard many les off.

On the second day of the same month they attacked the village, and on the third day about ten men went on shore. The villagers made their escape, so that the pirates could not take them. Having some time before made preparations to fortify Ma king yun,‡ they now retired to it. The pirates knowing that the villagers were well provided for defence, waited until (14 v.) they had every thing ready. On the fourth the pirates landed ; it was in vain that the villagers opposed them, they had two men

---

* *Laou ya, Lnou ya kang*, the mountain ridge of Laou ya, is fifteen le from the town of the third rank called *Shih ching*. Shih ching hëen belongs to the district Kaou chow foo. Kwang tung tsuen too, 16v. 9r.

† Crackers made of gunpowder, and the gong, are used at every Chinese festival.

‡ The name of a temple which Europeans commonly call a Pagoda.

wounded, and were finally defeated. The Go- 1810.
vernor-general ordered Ching chuy loo to proceed at the head of a large body of soldiers to
the town Shun tih, and prepare for an attack.
Meeting the pirates at Ke chow, the Major
attacking them on a sudden, the pirates sustained a great loss, and returned to their vessels.
The Major also was struck by a shot from a
musket. There were daily skirmishes at the
neighbouring places; the inhabitants were generally defeated and ran away. The Major
Loo came with his forces and placed them on
the sea-coast behind the intrenchments of Sin
ne, to protect them against the fire of the
enemy. The guns of the pirates were directed
against the place, the bullets fell in Sin ne, but
without hurting any one, which again calmed
and encouraged the inhabitants. The pirates (15 r.)
coming a second time before Ke chow and Ta
leang, and not being able to accomplish their
designs, thought fit to retire.

The wife of Ching yïh, on seeing that O po tae
was made a government officer after his submission, and that he did well, thought also of making

1810. her submission. " I am," said she, " ten times stronger than O po tae, and government would perhaps, if I submit, act towards me as they did with O po tae." But remembering their former crimes, and the opposition they made to many officers, these pirates were apprehensive and felt undetermined in their resolutions. A rumour (15 v.) went about, that the red squadron wished to tender their submission, and, in consequence, the vigilant magistrates hearing of this, invited them to do so. The magistrate of Tsze ne, Yu che chang, ordered a certain Fei hëung chow to make enquiries about the matter. Fei hëung chow was a physician of Macao, and being well acquainted with the pirates, he was not in need of any introduction to obtain access to them. This was the ground on which Yu chi chang particularly selected him, when he tried to bring the pirates to submission.

When Fei hëung chow came to Paou, he said: "Friend Paou, do you know why I come to you?"

Paou.—"Thou hast committed some crime and comest to me for protection ?"

Chow.—" By no means."

Paou.—" You will then know, how it stands 1810. concerning the report about our submission, if it is true or false ?"

Chow.—" You are again wrong here, Sir.* What are you in comparison with O po tae?"

Paou.—" Who is bold enough to compare me (16 r) with O po tae?"

Chow.—" I know very well that O po tae could not come up to you, Sir; but I mean only, that since O po tae has made his submission, since he has got his pardon and been created a government officer,—how would it be, if you with your whole crew should also submit, and if his Excellency should desire to treat you in the same manner, and to give you the same rank as O po tae? Your submission would produce more joy to government than the submission of O po tae. You should not wait for wisdom to act wisely; you should make up your mind to submit to the government with all your followers.

* Keun in Chinese, Kwa according to the Canton pronunciation. It is true it is somewhat awkward to speak of Madam Ching and Mr. Paou, but it may be remarked that the Chinese use their familiar expressions *foo* or *keun* in the same manner as we use Mr. and Mrs.

1810. I will assist you in every respect,—it would be
the means of securing your own happiness and
the lives of all your adherents."

Chang paou remained like a statue without
motion, and Fei hëung chow went on to say :
(16 v.) " You should think about this affair in time,
and not stay till the last moment. Is it not
clear that O po tae, since you could not agree
together, has joined government. He being
enraged against you, will fight, united with the
forces of the government, for your destruction ;
and who could help you, so that you might
overcome your enemies ? If O po tae could
before vanquish you quite alone, how much
more can he now when he is united with government ? O po tae will then satisfy his hatred
against you, and you yourself will soon be taken
either at Wei chow or at Neaou chow. If the
merchant-vessels of Hwy chaou, the boats of
Kwang chow, and all the fishing-vessels unite
(17 r.) together to surround and attack you in the open
sea, you will certainly have enough to do. But
even supposing they should not attack you, you
will soon feel the want of provisions, to sustain

you and all your followers. It is always wisdom 1810.
to provide before things happen ; stupidity and
folly never think about future events. It is too
late to reflect upon events when things have
happene ; you should, therefore, consider this
matter in time !"

Paou held a deliberation with the wife of
Ching yĭh, and she said : " The Doctor Chow
is certainly right in all that he says ; Paou may
agree with him." Paou then asked the Doctor :
" Have you any commission about this matter,
or not ?" The Doctor answered, " How could
I trifle with the sentiments of government ; this
would be declared an improper behaviour. (17 v.)
Neither can I see through the intentions of
the wife of Ching yĭh nor through those of the
officers of government ; you can clear up all
doubts, if you will collect your vessels about
Shao kĕŏ, outside the Bocca Tigris, you may
yourself hear the orders."

Paou consented to this proposal, and the Doctor
returned to Yu che chang. Yu che chang acquainted the Governor-general with this matter.
The general was anxious to meet the pirates and

R

1810. to clear the western passage, as he had already
cleared the eastern passage; he therefore was
very happy at hearing the offer of surrender.
The magistrate of Tsze ne, Yu che chang, took
the government proclamation and went to the
pirates to see how things stood. The wife of
Ching yïh on seeing Yu che chang, ordered
Chang paou to prepare a banquet. Chang paou
explained his intentions. Yu che chang remained the whole night on board ship, and
stated that government was willing to pardon
(18 r.) them, and that they had nothing to fear after
having made their submission. Paou was very
much rejoiced at this; and on the next morning
he went with Yu che chang to inspect the vessels, and ordered all the captains to pay their
respects to the government officer. The wife of
Ching yïh stated to Yu che chang that it was
her earnest wish to submit to government; and
Chang paou himself assured the officer of his firm
intention to surrender without the least deceit.
The governor then ordered Yu che chang to visit
the pirates a second time, accompanied by Pang
noo, in order to settle all with them regarding

their submission.   Chang paou requested that 1810.
those pirates who had been condemned to death
should be placed in ten vessels, in order that he
might ransom them.   Yu che chang reported
this, and the Governor said : " It shall be so,
whether Chang paou submit himself or not.
But being exceedingly desirous that the pirates
may surrender, I will go myself and state my
intentions, to clear up all doubts."

He ordered the Doctor Fei hëung chow to ac-
quaint the pirates with his design.   The Gover- (18 v.)
nor-general then embarked in a vessel with
Pang noo and Yu che chang to meet the pirates,
where they were assembled ;—their vessels occupied a space of about ten le.   On hearing
that the Governor-general was coming, they
hoisted their flags, played on their instruments,
and fired their guns, so that the smoke rose in
clouds, and then went to meet him.   From the
other side the people all became alarmed, and
the Governor-general himself was very much
astonished, being yet uncertain what could be the
meaning of all this alarm.   Chang paou, accompanied by the wife of Ching yïh, by Pang chang

1810. ching, Leang po paou, and Soo puh gaou, mounted the governor's ship, and rushed through the smoke to the place where the governor was stationed. The Governor-general on seeing Paou and his followers falling on their hands and knees, that (19 r.) they shed tears on account of their former crimes, and sued penitently for their lives, was induced by his extreme kindness to declare that he would again point out to the rebels the road to virtue. Paou and his followers were extremely affected, knocked their heads on the ground, and swore that they were ready to suffer death. But the Governor replied : " Since you are ready to submit yourselves with a true heart, I will lay aside all arms and disperse the soldiery ; to say it in one word, I give you three days to make up a list of your vessels and all your other possessions. Are you satisfied with this proposal or not ?" Paou and his followers said " *yes, yes,*" and retired accordingly.

It happened that about the same time some Portuguese vessels were about to enter the Bocca Tigris, and that some large men-of-war took their station at the same place. The pirates became exceedingly alarmed at this fleet, and 1810. apprehended that the Governor had made an agreement with the foreign vessels to destroy them. They immediately weighed their anchors and steered away.   On seeing the pirates run- (19 v.) ning away, Pang noo, Yu che chang, and the others, not knowing what could be the reason of all this, became afraid that they might have changed their mind, and that an attack on the Governor was contemplated. All parties became frightened that the meeting had failed, and made preparations to go off. The inhabitants of the neighbouring country hearing of this, ran away, and the Governor-general himself went back to Canton.

When the pirates ascertained that the foreign vessels were traders going into the river, and that the Governor-general had no communication with them, they again became pacified.   But considering that the Governor-general went back to Canton without the business of their submission being quite settled, they held a consultation together and Paou said: " His Excellency is gone back, and probably in doubt about our

1810. intentions ; if we tender our submission again,
(20 r.) his Excellency will not trust us, and if we do
not submit we shall insult the good intentions of
government.   What is to be done under these
circumstances ?"

The wife of Ching yĭh said : " His Excellency
behaved himself towards us in a candid manner,
and in like manner we must behave towards
him.   We being driven about on the ocean,
without having any fixed habitation ;—pray let
us go to Canton to inform government, to state
the reason of the recoiling waves, to clear up all
doubts, and to agree on what day or in what
place we shall make our submission.   His Excellency may then explain to us whether he will
come a second time to accept our submission,
or whether he will decline it."

The whole crew was of opinion, that " the
designs of government were unfathomable, and
that it would not be prudent to go so hastily on."
But the wife of Ching yĭh replied : " If his
(20 v.) Excellency, a man of the highest rank, could
come quickly to us quite alone, why should I a
mean woman not go to the officers of govern-

ment? If there be any danger in it, I will take 1810.
it on myself, no person among you will be required to trouble himself about it."

Leang po paou said: " If the wife of Ching
yïh goes, we must fix a time when she shall
return. If this time be past without our obtaining any certain information, we should collect all our forces and go before Canton.* This
is my opinion; if you think otherwise, let us retire; but let me hear your opinion?" They all
answered: " Friend Paou, we have heard thy
opinion, but we think it rather better to wait for
the news here on the water, than to send the
wife of Ching yïh alone to be killed." This was
the result of the consultation.

Yu che chang and Fei hëung chow, on seeing (21 r.
that nothing was settled about the submission
to government, became alarmed, and sent Chao
kaou yuen to Chang paou to enquire what was
the reason of it. On learning that they ran
away from fear of the foreign vessels, Yu che
chang and Fei hëung chow made another visit to
the pirates, in order to correct this mistake.

* In the text is only Chow (1355); but I think it must here be
taken for the city or town of Canton.

1810. " If you let slip this opportunity," said they,
" you will not be accepted, perhaps, should
you even be willing to make your submission.
The kindness of his Excellency is immense like
the sea, without being mixed with any falsehood ; we will pledge ourselves that the wife of
Ching yĭh, if she would go, would be received
with kindness."

The wife of Ching yĭh said : " You speak
well, gentlemen ; I will go myself to Canton
with some other ladies, accompanied by Yu che
chang."

Chang paou said, laughingly : " I am sorry his
(21 v.) Excellency should have any doubt regarding us,
for this reason, therefore, we will send our wives
to settle the affair for us."

When the wives and children appeared before
him, the Governor-general said to them : " You
did not change your mind, but ran away, being
deceived by a false impression ; for this reason
I will take no notice of it.   I am commanded
by the humanity of his Majesty's government
not to kill but to pardon you ; I therefore now
pardon Chang paou."

CHINESE PIRATES. 89

In consequence of this, Chang paou came with 1810.
his wives and children, and with the wife of Ching
yïh, at Foo yung shao near the town of Hëang shan
to submit himself to government. Every vessel
was provided with pork and wine, and every
man received at the same time a bill for a certain quantity of money. Those who wished it,
could join the military force of government for
pursuing the remaining pirates ; and those who
objected, dispersed and withdrew into the country. This is the manner by which the red squadron of the pirates was pacified.

After the submission of Chang paou, the Go- (22 r.)
vernor-general said: " Now that we have cleared,
both the eastern and the middle passage, we are
ready to reduce the pirates of the western passage. He held a consultation about this matter
with the deputy-governor Han fung, and then
ordered the principal officer of the public gra-
nary, Mwan ching che, and the military com-
mandant of Luy chow foo, Kang chow foo, and
Këung chow foo, called Chuh url kang gïh,* to

* About the towns which are mentioned in our text, the
reader may compare the notes to the first book. It is quite impos-

S

1810. proceed at the head of the forces and drive the
pirates away.   It was presumed that they would
retire more westerly to Annam ; a message was
therefore sent to the king of that country to
have ready an armed force to repulse the pirates,
whenever they should appear on the rivers or
on the mainland.* Chang paou was ordered on
the vanguard.

sible to ascertain by the text alone if there was only one military
officer appointed for all these places or not.   In the latter case it
would be necessary to read Chuh url and Kang gĭh ; but we see by
p. 95 that Chuh url kang gĭh is the name of *one* commander.

    * Tung king and Cochin-China now form one empire, under
the name of Annam or Annan.   The king of this country acknowledges the supremacy of the Chinese emperor, and sends
every year a tribute to Pekin.   The time of the reign of every
king is known by an honorary title, like that of the emperors
of China.   The honorary title of the period of the reigning king, to whom the message was sent, was *Kea lung*
(good fortune), the younger brother of *King ching*, called by his
proper name *Fŭh ying* (according to the Chinese Mandarin pronunciation): he is often mentioned in the beginning of the first book
of our *History of the Pirates*.   The king, commonly called Kea
lung, died Feb. 1820, in the 19th year of his reign.   His son,
who still reigns, mounted the throne on the third day after his
father's death, assuming the words *Ming ming* (Illustrious fortune),
as the designation of his reign. See the " Indo-Chinese Gleaner,"
vol. i. p. 360.   It was falsely reported that Ming ming was murdered some days after his succession to the throne (Indo-Chinese
Gleaner, l. c. p. 416), and this report is stated as a fact in the
generally very accurate work, Hamilton's East-India Gazetteer,

By the tenth day of the fourth moon the 1810. vessels and the crew were quite ready, and fell in on the twelfth of the same month with the yellow flag quite alone at Tse sing yang. Our commander valiantly attacked this squadron, and defeated it entirely. The captain Le tsung (22v.) chaou, with three hundred and ninety of his people, were taken prisoners. Meeting a division of the green flag, consisting of ten pirate vessels, our commander attacked them. The pirates being afraid, ran away; but our commander pursued after and killed them. Those who were taken alive were beheaded.

On the tenth day of the fifth moon the Governor-general went to Kaou chow to make preparations for fighting. Our commander pursued after the pirates with a great and strong body of troops; he met Neaou shĭh url at Tan chow, and they fought a great battle. Neaou shĭh url saw that he was not strong enough to withstand

---

vol. i. p. 430. The reader may find some interesting particulars concerning the present state of Cochin-China, in the Canton Register 1829, No. 13. Chinese influence seems to be now predominating in that country.

1810. them, and tried to escape; but the Major, Fei teaou hwang,* gave orders to surround the pi-

(23 r.) rates. They fought from seven o'clock in the morning till one at noon, burnt ten vessels, and killed an immense number of the pirates. Neaou shǐh url was so weakened that he could scarcely make any opposition. On perceiving this through the smoke, Chang paou mounted on a sudden the vessel of the pirate, and cried out: " I Chang paou am come," and at the same moment he cut some pirates to pieces; the remainder were then hardly dealt with. Paou addressed himself in an angry tone to Neaou shǐh url, and said : " I advise you to submit, will you not follow my advice, what have you to say ?" Neaou shǐh url was struck with amazement, and his courage left him. Leang po paou advanced and bound him, and the whole crew were then taken captives.

Seeing that Neaou shǐh url was taken, his elder brother Yew kwei would have run away in all haste ; but the admirals Tung and Tsuen (23 v.) mow sun pursued, attacked, and took him

---

* *Teaou* (10044) in our text is written with a vulgar character.

prisoner. The government officers Kung gao 1810.
and Hoo tso chaou took the younger brother of
Neaou shïh url, called Mih yew keih, and all the
others then made their submission. Not long
after this the *Scourge of the eastern ocean* surrendered voluntarily, on finding himself unable
to withstand; the *Frog's meal* withdrew to
Luzon or Manilla. On the twentieth of the
same month, the Governor-general came to
Luy chow, and every officer was ordered to
bring his prizes into the harbour or bay of
Man ke. There were taken fighting five hundred pirates, men and women ; three thousand
four hundred and sixty made their submission ;
there were eighty-six vessels, two hundred and
ninety-one guns, and one thousand three hundred
and seventy-two pieces of various military
weapons. The Governor-general ordered one
of his officers to kill* the pirate Neaou shïh url
with eight others outside the northern entrance
of Hae kăng hëen,† and to behead Hwang hŏ (24 r.)

* Chih (Kang he under radical 112. B. vii. p. 19 r.) seems to
indicate that they have been put to death by cutting one member
after another.
† Hae kăng is a town of the third rank and dependent on the

1810. with one hundred and nineteen of his followers The *Scourge of the eastern sea* submitting himself voluntarily was not put to death.

There was much talk concerning a man at Hae kăng hëen, whose crime was of such a nature that it could not be overlooked. When this man was carried away to suffer death, his wife pressed him in her arms, and said with great demonstration of sorrow, " Because thou didst not follow my words, it is even thus. I said before what is now come to pass, that thou fighting as a pirate against the officers of government would be taken and put to death. This fills my mind with sorrow. If thou hadst made thy submission like O po tae and Chang paou, thou (24 v.) wouldst have been pardoned like them; thou art now given up to the law, not by any power of man, but by the will of fate." Having finished these words, she cried exceedingly. The Governor-general was moved by these

---

district metropolis Luy chow foo   Luy chow foo is westerly from Canton 1380 le. Hae kang is near to its district metropolis *Kwang tung tsuen too*, p. v. 9 v. See the Notes, p 9, of this work.

words, and commuted the punishment of that 1810. pirate into imprisonment.

In this manner the western passage was cleared from the green, yellow, and blue squadrons, and smaller divisions. The rest of the pirates, who remained about Hae kăng, at Hae fung, at Suy ke and Hŏ poo, were gradually destroyed.* The Governor-general ordered Chuh url kang gĭh and Mwan ching che to go with an armed force and sweep away those pirates, who hid themselves in the recesses of Wei chow and Neaou chow. And thus finished this meritorious act of the *Pacification of the pirates.*

By an edict of the " Son of Heaven," the (25ir.) Governor-general of Kwang tung and Kwang se

* *Hae fung* is a town of the third rank, and dependent on the district metropolis Hwy chow foo. It is in a north-east direction from its district metropolis 300 le. Its area contains forty le, and pays 17,266 leang in taxes.

Suy ke is a town of the third rank, and dependent upon the district metropolis Luy chow foo; distance from Luy chow foo in a northerly direction 180 le.

Hŏ poo is a town of the third rank, and dependant on the district metropolis Lëen chow foo. This town is near to the district metropolis, has an area of thirty le, and pays 7,458 leang in taxes. *Kwang tung tsuen too*, p. 6 r. p. 9 v.

1810. *Pih, ling* was recompensed for his merits.   He
was created a secondary guardian of the Prince,
allowed to wear peacock's-feathers with two
eyes, and favoured with an hereditary title.
The services of the different officers and commanders were taken into consideration, and
they received adequate recompenses. Chang
paou was appointed to the rank of Major; Tung
hae pa, or, the Scourge of the eastern sea, and
all others, were pardoned, with the permission
to retire wherever they wished.   From that period till now ships pass and repass in tranquillity.
All is quiet on the rivers, the four seas are tran-
quil, and people live in peace and plenty.

APPENDIX.

———•———

THE Translator supposing that the readers of the *History of the Chinese Pirates* might perhaps find it interesting to compare the account of the followers of *The wife of Ching yih,* drawn up by an European, with the statements of the non-official Chinese historian; he has therefore thought fit to subjoin a *Narrative of the captivity and treatment amongst the Ladrones,* written by Mr. Richard Glasspoole, of the Hon. Company's ship *Marquis of Ely,* and published in *Wilkinson's Travels to China.* The Translator in vain endeavoured to obtain another Narrative, regarding the Chinese pirates, which is said to be printed in an English periodical.

A brief Narrative of my captivity and treatment amongst the Ladrones.

On the 17th of September 1809, the Honourable Company's ship Marquis of Ely anchored under the Island of *Sam Chow,* in China, about twelve English miles from Macao, where I was ordered to proceed in

T

one of our cutters to procure a pilot, and also to land
the purser with the packet. I left the ship at 5 P.M.
with seven men under my command, well armed. It
blew a fresh gale from the N. E. We arrived at Macao
at 9 P.M , where I delivered the packet to Mr. Roberts,
and sent the men with the boat's sails to sleep under
the Company's Factory, and left the boat in charge of
one of the Compradore's men; during the night the
gale increased.—At half-past three in the morning I
went to the beach, and found the boat on shore half-
filled with water, in consequence of the man having left
her. I called the people, and baled her out; found
she was considerably damaged, and very leaky. At
half-past 5 A.M., the ebb-tide making, we left Macao
with vegetables for the ship.

One of the Compradore's men who spoke English
went with us for the purpose of piloting the ship to
Lintin, as the Mandarines, in consequence of a late
disturbance at Macao, would not grant chops for the
regular pilots. I had every reason to expect the ship
in the roads, as she was preparing to get under weigh
when we left her; but on our rounding Cabaretta-
Point, we saw her five or six miles to leeward, under
weigh, standing on the starboard-tack: it was then
blowing fresh at N. E. Bore up, and stood towards
her; when about a cable's-length to windward of her,
she tacked; we hauled our wind and stood after her.

A hard squall then coming on, with a strong tide and heavy swell against us, we drifted fast to leeward, and the weather being hazy, we soon lost sight of the ship. Struck our masts, and endeavoured to pull; finding our efforts useless, set a reefed foresail and mizen, and stood towards a country-ship at anchor under the land to leeward of Cabaretta-Point. When within a quarter of a mile of her she weighed and made sail, leaving us in a very critical situation, having no anchor, and drifting bodily on the rocks to leeward. Struck the masts: after four or five hours hard pulling, succeeded in clearing them.

At this time not a ship in sight; the weather clearing up, we saw a ship to leeward, hull down, shipped our masts, and made sail towards her; she proved to be the Honourable Company's ship Glatton. We made signals to her with our handkerchiefs at the mast-head, she unfortunately took no notice of them, but tacked and stood from us. Our situation was now truly distressing, night closing fast, with a threatening appearance, blowing fresh, with hard rain and a heavy sea; our boat very leaky, without a compass, anchor or provisions, and drifting fast on a lee-shore, surrounded with dangerous rocks, and inhabited by the most barbarous pirates. I close-reefed my sails, and kept tack and tack 'till day-light, when we were happy to find we had drifted very little to leeward of our situation in the evening. The night was very dark, with constant hard squalls and heavy rain.

Tuesday the 19th no ships in sight. About ten o'clock in the morning it fell calm, with very hard rain and a heavy swell;—struck our masts and pulled, not being able to see the land, steered by the swell. When the weather broke up, found we had drifted several miles to leeward. During the calm a fresh breeze springing up, made sail, and endeavoured to reach the weather-shore, and anchor with six muskets we had lashed together for that purpose. Finding the boat made no way against the swell and tide, bore up for a bay to leeward, and anchored about one A.M. close under the land in five or six fathoms water, blowing fresh, with hard rain.

Wednesday the 20th at day-light, supposing the flood-tide making, weighed and stood over to the weather-land, but found we were drifting fast to leeward. About ten o'clock perceived two Chinese boats steering for us. Bore up, and stood towards them, and made signals to induce them to come within hail; on nearing them, they bore up, and passed to leeward of the islands. The Chinese we had in the boat advised me to follow them, and he would take us to Macao by the leeward passage. I expressed my fears of being taken by the Ladrones. Our ammunition being wet, and the muskets rendered useless, we had nothing to defend ourselves with but cutlasses, and in too distressed a situation to make much resistance with them, having been constantly wet, and eat nothing but a few green oranges for three days.

As our present situation was a hopeless one, and the man assured me there was no fear of encountering any Ladrones, I complied with his request, and stood in to leeward of the islands, where we found the water much smoother, and apparently a direct passage to Macao. We continued pulling and sailing all day. At six o'clock in the evening I discovered three large boats at anchor in a bay to leeward. On seeing us they weighed and made sail towards us. The Chinese said they were Ladrones, and that if they captured us they would most certainly put us all to death! Finding they gained fast on us, struck the masts, and pulled head to wind for five or six hours. The tide turning against us, anchored close under the land to avoid being seen. Soon after we saw the boats pass us to leeward.

Thursday the 21st, at day-light, the flood making, weighed and pulled along shore in great spirits, expecting to be at Macao in two or three hours, as by the Chinese account it was not above six or seven miles distant. After pulling a mile or two perceived several people on shore, standing close to the beach; they were armed with pikes and lances. I ordered the interpreter to hail them, and ask the most direct passage to Macao.

They said if we came on shore they would inform us; not liking their hostile appearance I did not think proper to comply with the request. Saw a large fleet of boats at anchor close under the opposite shore. Our interpreter said they were fishing-boats, and that by going there we should not only get provisions, but a pilot also to take us to Macao.

I bore up, and on nearing them perceived there were some large vessels, very full of men, and mounted with several guns. I hesitated to approach nearer; but the Chinese assuring me they were Mandarine junks* and salt-boats, we stood close to one of them, and asked the way to Macao? They gave no answer, but made some signs to us to go in shore. We passed on, and a large row-boat pulled after us; she soon came along-side, when about twenty savage-looking villains, who were stowed at the bottom of the boat, leaped on board us. They were armed with a short sword in each hand, one of which they laid on our necks, and the other pointed to our breasts, keeping their eyes fixed on their officer, waiting his signal to cut or desist. Seeing we were incapable of making any resistance, he sheathed his sword, and the others immediately followed his example. They then dragged us into their boat, and carried us on board one of their junks, with the most savage demonstrations of joy, and as we supposed,

* *Junk* is the Canton pronunciation of *chuen*, ship.

to torture and put us to a cruel death. When on board the junk, they searched all our pockets, took the handkerchiefs from our necks, and brought heavy chains to chain us to the guns.

At this time a boat came, and took me, with one of my men and the interpreter, on board the chief's vessel. I was then taken before the chief. He was seated on deck, in a large chair, dressed in purple silk, with a black turban on He appeared to be about thirty years of age, a stout commanding-looking man. He took me by the coat, and drew me close to him; then questioned the interpreter very strictly, asking who we were, and what was our business in that part of the country. I told him to say we were Englishmen in distress, having been four days at sea without provisions. This he would not credit, but said we were bad men, and that he would put us all to death; and then ordered some men to put the interpreter to the torture until he confessed the truth.

Upon this occasion, a Ladrone, who had been once to England and spoke a few words of English, came to the chief, and told him we were really Englishmen, and that we had plenty of money, adding, that the buttons on my coat were gold. The chief then ordered us some coarse brown rice, of which we made a tolerable meal, having eat nothing for nearly four days, except a few green oranges. During our repast, a number of La-

drones crowded round us, examining our clothes and
hair, and giving us every possible annoyance. Several
of them brought swords, and laid them on our necks,
making signs that they would soon take us on shore,
and cut us in pieces, which I am sorry to say was the
fate of some hundreds during my captivity.

I was now summoned before the chief, who had been
conversing with the interpreter; he said I must write
to my captain, and tell him, if he did not send an hundred thousand dollars for our ransom, in ten days he
would put us all to death. In vain did I assure him it
was useless writing unless he would agree to take a
much smaller sum; saying we were all poor men, and
the most we could possibly raise would not exceed two
thousand dollars. Finding that he was much exasperated at my expostulations, I embraced the offer of
writing to inform my commander of our unfortunate
situation, though there appeared not the least proba-
bility of relieving us. They said the letter should be
conveyed to Macao in a fishing-boat, which would
bring an answer in the morning. A small boat accordingly came alongside, and took the letter.

About six o'clock in the evening they gave us some
rice and a little salt fish, which we eat, and they made
signs for us to lay down on the deck to sleep; but such
numbers of Ladrones were constantly coming from different vessels to see us, and examine our clothes and

hair, they would not allow us a moment's quiet. They were particularly anxious for the buttons of my coat, which were new, and as they supposed gold. I took it off, and laid it on the deck to avoid being disturbed by them; it was taken away in the night, and I saw it on the next day stripped of its buttons.

About nine o'clock a boat came and hailed the chief's vessel; he immediately hoisted his mainsail, and the fleet weighed apparently in great confusion. They worked to windward all night and part of the next day, and anchored about one o'clock in a bay under the island of Lantow, where the head admiral of Ladrones was lying at anchor, with about two hundred vessels and a Portuguese brig they had captured a few days before, and murdered the captain and part of the crew.

Saturday the 23d, early in the morning, a fishing-boat came to the fleet to inquire if they had captured an European boat; being answered in the affirmative, they came to the vessel I was in. One of them spoke a few words of English, and told me he had a Ladrone-pass, and was sent by Captain Kay in search of us; I was rather surprised to find he had no letter. He appeared to be well acquainted with the chief, and remained in his cabin smoking opium, and playing cards all the day.*

* The pirates had many other intimate acquaintances on shore, like Doctor *Chow* of Macao.

In the evening I was summoned with the interpreter before the chief. He questioned us in a much milder tone, saying, he now believed we were Englishmen, a people he wished to be friendly with ; and that if our captain would lend him seventy thousand dollars 'till he returned from his cruize up the river, he would repay him, and send us all to Macao. I assured him it was useless writing on those terms, and unless our ransom was speedily settled, the English fleet would sail, and render our enlargement altogether ineffectual. He remained determined, and said if it were not sent, he would keep us, and make us fight, or put us to death. I accordingly wrote, and gave my letter to the man belonging to the boat before mentioned. He said he could not return with an answer in less than five days.

The chief now gave me the letter I wrote when first taken. I have never been able to ascertain his reasons for detaining it, but suppose he dare not negotiate for our ransom without orders from the head admiral, who I understood was sorry at our being captured. He said the English ships would join the mandarines and attack them.* He told the chief that captured us, to dispose of us as he pleased.

---

* The pirates were always afraid of this. We find the following statement concerning the Chinese pirates, taken from the records in the East-India House, and printed in Appendix C. to the *Report relative to the trade with the East-Indies*

Monday the 24th, it blew a strong gale, with constant hard rain; we suffered much from the cold and wet, being obliged to remain on deck with no covering but an old mat, which was frequently taken from us in the night, by the Ladrones who were on watch. During the night the Portuguese who were left in the brig murdered the Ladrones that were on board of her, cut the cables, and fortunately escaped through the darkness of the night. I have since been informed they run her on shore near Macao.

Tuesday the 25th, at day-light in the morning, the fleet, amounting to about five hundred sail of different sizes, weighed, to proceed on their intended cruize up the rivers, to levy contributions on the towns and villages. It is impossible to describe what were my feelings

<hr/>

and China, in the sessions 1820 and 1821 (reprinted 1829), p 387.

" In the year 1808, 1809, and 1810, the Canton river was so infested with pirates, who were also in such force, that the Chinese government made an attempt to subdue them, but failed. The pirates totally destroyed the Chinese force; ravaged the river in every direction; threatened to attack the city of Canton, and destroyed many towns and villages on the banks of the river; and killed or carried off, to serve as Ladrones, several thousands of inhabitants.

" These events created an alarm extremely prejudicial to the commerce of Canton, and compelled the Company's supercargoes to fit out a small country ship to cruize for a short time against the pirates."

at this critical time, having received no answers to my letters, and the fleet under-way to sail,—hundreds of miles up a country never visited by Europeans, there to remain probably for many months, which would render all opportunities of negotiating for our enlargement totally ineffectual; as the only method of communication is by boats, that have a pass from the Ladrones, and they dare not venture above twenty miles from Macao, being obliged to come and go in the night, to avoid the Mandarines; and if these boats should be detected in having any intercourse with the Ladrones, they are immediately put to death, and all their relations, though they had not joined in the crime,* share in the punishment, in order that not a single person of their families should be left to imitate their crimes or revenge their death. This severity renders communication both dangerous and expensive; no boat would venture out for less than a hundred Spanish dollars

Wednesday the 26th, at day-light, we passed in sight of our ships at anchor under the island of Chun Po. The chief then called me, pointed to the ships, and told the interpreter to tell us to look at them, for we should never see them again. About noon we entered a river

* That the whole family must suffer for the crime of one individual, seems to be the most cruel and foolish law of the whole Chinese criminal code.

to the westward of the Bogue,* three or four miles from the entrance. We passed a large town situated on the side of a beautiful hill, which is tributary to the Ladrones; the inhabitants saluted them with songs as they passed.

The fleet now divided into two squadrons (the red and the black)† and sailed up different branches of the river. At midnight the division we were in anchored close to an immense hill, on the top of which a number of fires were burning, which at day-light I perceived proceeded from a Chinese camp At the back of the hill was a most beautiful town, surrounded by water, and embellished with groves of orange-trees. The chop-house (custom-house)‡ and a few cottages were immediately plundered, and burnt down; most of the inhabitants, however, escaped to the camp.

The Ladrones now prepared to attack the town with a formidable force, collected in row-boats from the dif-

* The Hoo mun, or Bocca Tigris.

† We know by the "History of the Chinese Pirates," that these "wasps of the ocean," to speak with *Yuen tsze yung lun,* were originally divided into six squadrons.

‡ In the barbarous Chinese-English spoken at Canton, all things are indiscriminately called *chop.* You hear of a chop-house, chop-boat, tea-chop, Chaou-chaou-chop, etc. To give a bill or agreement on making a bargain is in Chinese called *chă tan ;* chă in the pronunciation of Canton is *chop,* which is then applied to any writing whatever. See Dr. Morrison's English and Chinese Dictionary under the word *chop.*

ferent vessels. They sent a messenger to the town,
demanding a tribute of ten thousand dollars annually,
saying, if these terms were not complied with, they
would land, destroy the town, and murder all the inhabitants; which they would certainly have done, had
the town laid in a more advantageous situation for their
purpose; but being placed out of the reach of their
shot, they allowed them to come to terms. The inhabitants agreed to pay six thousand dollars, which they
were to collect by the time of our return down the
river. This finesse had the desired effect, for during
our absence they mounted a few guns on a hill, which
commanded the passage, and gave us in lieu of the
dollars a warm salute on our return.

October the 1st, the fleet weighed in the night'
dropped by the tide up the river, and anchored very
quietly before a town surrounded by a thick wood.
Early in the morning the Ladrones assembled in row-
boats, and landed; then gave a shout, and rushed into
the town, sword in hand. The inhabitants fled to the
adjacent hills, in numbers apparently superior to the
Ladrones. We may easily imagine to ourselves the
horror with which these miserable people must be
seized, on being obliged to leave their homes, and every
thing dear to them. It was a most melancholy sight to
see women in tears, clasping their infants in their arms,
and imploring mercy for them from those brutal

robbers! The old and the sick, who were unable to fly, or to make resistance, were either made prisoners or most inhumanly butchered! The boats continued passing and repassing from the junks to the shore, in quick succession, laden with booty, and the men besmeared with blood! Two hundred and fifty women, and several children, were made prisoners, and sent on board different vessels. They were unable to escape with the men, owing to that abominable practice of cramping their feet: several of them were not able to move without assistance, in fact, they might all be said to totter, rather than walk. Twenty of these poor women were sent on board the vessel I was in; they were hauled on board by the hair, and treated in a most savage manner.

When the chief came on board, he questioned them respecting the circumstances of their friends, and demanded ransoms accordingly, from six thousand to six hundred dollars each. He ordered them a berth on deck, at the after part of the vessel, where they had nothing to shelter them from the weather, which at this time was very variable,—the days excessively hot, and the nights cold, with heavy rains. The town being plundered of every thing valuable, it was set on fire, and reduced to ashes by the morning. The fleet remained here three days, negotiating for the ransom of the prisoners, and plundering the fish-tanks and

gardens.   During all this time, the Chinese never ven-
tured from the hills, though there were frequently not
more than a hundred Ladrones on shore at a time,
and I am sure the people on the hills exceeded ten
times that number.*

October the 5th, the fleet proceeded up another
branch of the river, stopping at several small villages to
receive tribute, which was generally paid in dollars,
sugar and rice, with a few large pigs roasted whole, as
presents for their joss (the idol they worship).* Every
person on being ransomed, is obliged to present him
with a pig, or some fowls, which the priest offers him
with prayers; it remains before him a few hours, and is
then divided amongst the crew. Nothing particular
occurred 'till the 10th, except frequent skirmishes on
shore between small parties of Ladrones and Chinese
soldiers. They frequently obliged my men to go on
shore, and fight with the muskets we had when taken,
which did great execution, the Chinese principally
using bows and arrows. They have match-locks, but
use them very unskilfully.

* The following is the *Character of the Chinese of Canton, as
given in ancient Chinese books :* " People of Canton are silly, light,
weak in body, and weak in mind, without any ability to fight on
land." The Indo-Chinese Gleaner, No. 19.

† *Joss* is a Chinese corruption of the Portuguese *Dios, God.*
The Joss, or idol, of which Mr. Glasspoole speaks in the *San po
shin,* which is spoken of in the work of Yuen tsze.

On the 10th, we formed a junction with the Black-squadron, and proceeded many miles up a wide and beautiful river, passing several ruins of villages that had been destroyed by the Black-squadron. On the 17th, the fleet anchored abreast four mud batteries, which defended a town, so entirely surrounded with wood that it was impossible to form any idea of its size. The weather was very hazy, with hard squalls of rain. The Ladrones remained perfectly quiet for two days. On the third day the forts commenced a brisk fire for several hours: the Ladrones did not return a single shot, but weighed in the night and dropped down the river.

The reasons they gave for not attacking the town, or returning the fire, were, that Joss had not promised them success. They are very superstitious, and consult their idol on all occasions. If his omens are good, they will undertake the most daring enterprizes.

The fleet now anchored opposite the ruins of the town where the women had been made prisoners. Here we remained five or six days, during which time about an hundred of the women were ransomed; the remainder were offered for sale amongst the Ladrones, for forty dollars each. The woman is considered the lawful wife of the purchaser, who would be put to death if he discarded her. Several of them leaped over-board and drowned themselves, rather than submit to such infamous degradation.*

The fleet then weighed and made sail down the river, to receive the ransom from the town before-mentioned. As we passed the hill, they fired several shot at us, but without effect. The Ladrones were much exasperated, and determined to revenge themselves; they dropped out of reach of their shot, and anchored. Every junk sent about a hundred men each on shore, to cut paddy, and destroy their orange-groves, which was most effectually performed for several miles down the river. During our stay here, they received information of nine boats lying up a creek, laden with paddy; boats were immediately dispatched after them.

Next morning these boats were brought to the fleet; ten or twelve men were taken in them. As these had made no resistance, the chief said he would allow them to become Ladrones, if they agreed to take the usual oaths before Joss. Three or four of them refused to comply, for which they were punished in the following cruel manner: their hands were tied behind their back, a rope from the mast-head rove through their arms, and hoisted three or four feet from the deck, and five or six men flogged them with three rattans twisted together 'till they were apparently dead; then hoisted

* Yuen tsze reported the memorable deed of the beautiful *Mei ying* at the end of the first book of his history.

them up to the mast-head, and left them hanging nearly an hour, then lowered them down, and repeated the punishment, 'till they died or complied with the oath.

October the 20th, in the night, an express-boat came with the information that a large mandarine fleet was proceeding up the river to attack us. The chief immediately weighed, with fifty of the largest vessels, and sailed down the river to meet them. About one in the morning they commenced a heavy fire till day-light, when an express was sent for the remainder of the fleet to join them: about an hour after a counter-order to anchor came, the mandarine-fleet having run. Two or three hours afterwards the chief returned with three captured vessels in tow, having sunk two, and eighty-three sail made their escape. The admiral of the mandarines blew his vessel up, by throwing a lighted match into the magazine as the Ladrones were boarding her; she ran on shore, and they succeeded in getting twenty of her guns.

In this action very few prisoners were taken: the men belonging to the captured vessels drowned themselves, as they were sure of suffering a lingering and cruel death if taken after making resistance. The admiral left the fleet in charge of his brother, the second in command, and proceeded with his own vessel towards Lantow. The fleet remained in this river, cutting paddy, and getting the necessary supplies.

On the 28th of October, I received a letter from
Captain Kay, brought by a fisherman, who had told
him he would get us all back for three thousand dollars.
He advised me to offer three thousand, and if not accepted, extend it to four; but not farther, as it was bad
policy to offer much at first : at the same time assuring
me we should be liberated, let the ransom be what it
would.   I offered the chief the three thousand, which
he disdainfully refused, saying he was not to be played
with; and unless they sent ten thousand dollars, and
two large guns, with several casks of gunpowder, he
would soon put us all to death.   I wrote to Captain
Kay, and informed him of the chief's determination,
requesting if an opportunity offered, to send us a shift
of clothes, for which it may be easily imagined we were
much distressed, having been seven weeks without a
shift; although constantly exposed to the weather, and
of course frequently wet.

On the first of November, the fleet sailed up a narrow
river, and anchored at night within two miles of a town
called Little Whampoa.   In front of it was a small
fort, and several mandarine vessels lying in the harbour.
The chief sent the interpreter to me, saying, I must
order my men to make cartridges and clean their
muskets, ready to go on shore in the morning.   I assured the interpreter I should give the men no such
orders, that they must please themselves.   Soon after

the chief came on board, threatening to put us all to a cruel death if we refused to obey his orders. For my own part I remained determined, and advised the men not to comply, as I thought by making ourselves useful we should be accounted too valuable.

A few hours afterwards he sent to me again, saying, that if myself and the quarter-master would assist them at the great guns, that if also the rest of the men went on shore and succeeded in taking the place, he would then take the money offered for our ransom, and give them twenty dollars for every Chinaman's head they cut off. To these proposals we cheerfully acceded, in hopes of facilitating our deliverance.

Early in the morning the forces intended for landing were assembled in row-boats, amounting in the whole to three or four thousand men. The largest vessels weighed, and hauled in shore, to cover the landing of the forces, and attack the fort and mandarine-vessels. About nine o'clock the action commenced, and continued with great spirit for nearly an hour, when the walls of the fort gave way, and the men retreated in the greatest confusion.

The mandarine vessels still continued firing, having blocked up the entrance of the harbour to prevent the Ladrone boats entering. At this the Ladrones were much exasperated, and about three hundred of them swam on shore, with a short sword lashed close under

each arm; they then ran along the banks of the river
'till they came a-breast of the vessels, and then swam
off again and boarded them. The Chinese thus attacked, leaped over-board, and endeavoured to reach
the opposite shore; the Ladrones followed, and cut the
greater number of them to pieces in the water. They
next towed the vessels out of the harbour, and attacked
the town with increased fury. The inhabitants fought
about a quarter of an hour, and then retreated to an
adjacent hill, from which they were soon driven with
great slaughter.

After this the Ladrones returned, and plundered the
town, every boat leaving it when laden. The Chinese
on the hills perceiving most of the boats were off, ral-
lied, and retook the town, after killing near two hundred
Ladrones. One of my men was unfortunately lost in
this dreadful massacre! The Ladrones landed a second
time, drove the Chinese out of the town, then reduced
it to ashes, and put all their prisoners to death, without
regarding either age or sex!

I must not omit to mention a most horrid (though
ludicrous) circumstance which happened at this place.
The Ladrones were paid by their chief ten dollars for
every Chinaman's head they produced. One of my
men turning the corner of a street was met by a Ladrone running furiously after a Chinese; he had a
drawn sword in his hand, and two Chinaman's heads

which he had cut off, tied by their tails, and slung round his neck. I was witness myself to some of them producing five or six to obtain payment ! ! !

On the 4th of November an order arrived from the admiral for the fleet to proceed immediately to Lantow, where he was lying with only two vessels, and three Portuguese ships and a brig constantly annoying him; several sail of mandarine vessels were daily expected. The fleet weighed and proceeded towards Lantow. On passing the island of Lintin, three ships and a brig gave chase to us. The Ladrones prepared to board; but night closing we lost sight of them : I am convinced they altered their course and stood from us. These vessels were in the pay of the Chinese government, and style themselves the Invincible Squadron, cruizing in the river Tigris to annihilate the Ladrones !

On the fifth, in the morning, the red squadron anchored in a bay under Lantow; the black squadron stood to the eastward. In this bay they hauled several of their vessels on shore to bream their bottoms and repair them.

In the afternoon of the 8th of November, four ships, a brig and a schooner came off the mouth of the bay. At first the pirates were much alarmed, supposing them to be English vessels come to rescue us. Some of them threatened to hang us to the mast-head for them to fire at; and with much difficulty we persuaded them that they were Portuguese. The Ladrones had only seven junks in a fit state for action; these they hauled outside, and moored them head and stern across the bay; and manned all the boats belonging to the repairing vessels ready for boarding.

The Portuguese observing these manœuvres hove to, and communicated by boats. Soon afterwards they made sail, each ship firing her broadside as she passed, but without effect, the shot falling far short: The Ladrones did not return a single shot, but waved their colours, and threw up rockets, to induce them to come further in, which they might easily have done, the outside junks lying in four fathoms water which I sounded myself: though the Portuguese in their letters to Macao, lamented there was not sufficient water for them to engage closer, but that they would certainly prevent their escaping before the mandarine fleet arrived!

On the 20th of November, early in the morning, discovered an immense fleet of mandarine vessels standing for the bay. On nearing us, they formed a line, and stood close in; each vessel as she discharged her guns tacked to join the rear and reload. They kept up a constant fire for about two hours, when one of their largest vessels was blown up by a firebrand thrown from a Ladrone junk; after which they kept at a more respectful distance, but continued firing without intermission 'till the 21st at night, when it fell calm.

The Ladrones towed out seven large vessels, with about two hundred row-boats to board them; but a breeze springing up, they made sail and escaped. The Ladrones returned into the bay, and anchored. The Portuguese and mandarines followed, and continued a heavy cannonading during that night and the next day. The vessel I was in had her foremast shot away, which they supplied very expeditiously by taking a mainmast from a smaller vessel.

On the 23d, in the evening, it again fell calm; the Ladrones towed out fifteen junks in two divisions, with the intention of surrounding them, which was nearly effected, having come up with and boarded one, when a breeze suddenly sprung up. The captured vessel mounted twenty-two guns. Most of her crew leaped overboard; sixty or seventy were taken immediately, cut to pieces and thrown into the river. Early in the morning the Ladrones returned into the bay, and anchored in the same situation as before. The Portuguese and mandarines followed, keeping up a constant fire. The Ladrones never returned a single shot, but always kept in readiness to board, and the Portuguese were careful never to allow them an opportunity.

On the 28th, at night, they sent in eight fire-vessels, which if properly constructed must have done great execution, having every advantage they could wish for to effect their purpose; a strong breeze and tide di-

rectly into the bay, and the vessels lying so close together that it was impossible to miss them.   On their first
appearance the Ladrones gave a general shout, supposing them to be mandarine vessels* on fire, but were
very soon convinced of their mistake.   They came very
regularly into the centre of the fleet, two and two,
burning furiously ; one of them came alongside of the
vessel I was in, but they succeeded in booming her off.
She appeared to be a vessel of about thirty tons ; her
hold was filled with straw and wood, and there were a
few small boxes of combustibles on her deck, which
exploded alongside of us without doing any damage.
The Ladrones, however, towed them all on shore, extinguished the fire, and broke them up for fire-wood.
The Portuguese claim the credit of constructing these
destructive machines, and actually sent a dispatch to
the Governor of Macao, saying they had destroyed at
least one-third of the Ladrones' fleet, and hoped soon
to effect their purpose by totally annihilating them.

On the 29th of November, the Ladrones being all
ready for sea, they weighed and stood boldly out,
bidding defiance to the invincible squadron and imperial fleet, consisting of ninety-three war-junks, six Portuguese ships, a brig, and a schooner.   Immediately the
Ladrones weighed, they made all sail.   The Ladrones
chased them two or three hours, keeping up a constant

* The *Chang lung* vessels.

fire; finding they did not come up with them, they hauled their wind and stood to the eastward.

Thus terminated the boasted blockade, which lasted nine days, during which time the Ladrones completed all their repairs. In this action not a single Ladrone vessel was destroyed, and their loss about thirty or forty men. An American was also killed, one of three that remained out of eight taken in a schooner. I had two very narrow escapes: the first, a twelve-pounder shot fell within three or four feet of me; another took a piece out of a small brass-swivel on which I was standing. The chief's wife* frequently sprinkled me with garlic-water, which they consider an effectual charm against shot. The fleet continued under sail all night, steering towards the eastward. In the morning they anchored in a large bay surrounded by lofty and barren mountains.

On the 2nd of December I received a letter from Lieutenant Maughn, commander of the Honourable Company's cruizer Antelope, saying that he had the ransom on board, and had been three days cruizing after us, and wished me to settle with the chief on the securest method of delivering it. The chief agreed to send us in a small gun-boat, 'till we came within sight

* Probably the wife of Ching yï'h, whose family name was Shïh, or stone.

of the Antelope; then the Compradore's boat was to
bring the ransom and receive us.

I was so agitated at receiving this joyful news, that
it was with considerable difficulty I could scrawl about
two or three lines to inform Lieutenant Maughn of the
arrangements I had made. We were all so deeply
affected by the gratifying tidings, that we seldom closed
our eyes, but continued watching day and night for the
boat. On the 6th she returned with Lieutenant
Maughn's answer, saying, he would respect any single
boat; but would not allow the fleet to approach him.
The chief then, according to his first proposal, ordered
a gun-boat to take us, and with no small degree of pleasure we left the Ladrone fleet about four o'clock in the
morning.

At one P.M. saw the Antelope under all sail, standing
toward us. The Ladrone boat immediately anchored,
and dispatched the Compradore's boat for the ransom,
saying, that if she approached nearer, they would return to the fleet; and they were just weighing when
she shortened sail, and anchored about two miles from
us. The boat did not reach her 'till late in the afternoon, owing to the tide's being strong against her. She
received the ransom and left the Antelope just before
dark. A mandarine boat that had been lying concealed under the land, and watching their manœuvres,
gave chace to her, and was within a few fathoms of

taking her, when she saw a light, which the Ladrones answered, and the Mandarine hauled off.

Our situation was now a most critical one; the ransom was in the hands of the Ladrones, and the Compradore dare not return with us for fear of a second attack from the mandarine boat. The Ladrones would not remain 'till morning, so we were obliged to return with them to the fleet.

In the morning the chief inspected the ransom, which consisted of the following articles: two bales of superfine scarlet cloth; two chests of opium; two casks of gunpowder; and a telescope; the rest in dollars. He objected to the telescope not being new; and said he should detain one of us 'till another was sent, or a hundred dollars in lieu of it. The Compradore however agreed with him for the hundred dollars.

Every thing being at length settled, the chief ordered two gun-boats to convey us near the Antelope; we saw her just before dusk, when the Ladrone boats left us. We had the inexpressible pleasure of arriving on board the Antelope at 7 P.M., where we were most cordially received, and heartily congratulated on our safe and happy deliverance from a miserable captivity, which we had endured for eleven weeks and three days.

(Signed)   RICHARD GLASSPOOLE.

CHINA, December 8th, 1809.

A few Remarks on the Origin, Progress, Manners,
and Customs of the Ladrones.

THE Ladrones are a disaffected race of Chinese, that
revolted against the oppressions of the mandarines.—
They first commenced their depredations on the
Western coast (Cochin-China), by attacking small trading vessels in row-boats, carrying from thirty to forty men
each.   They continued this system of piracy several
years; at length their successes, and the oppressive state
of the Chinese, had the effect of rapidly increasing their
numbers. Hundreds of fishermen and others flocked to
their standard ; and as their number increased they consequently became more desperate.   They blockaded all
the principal rivers, and attacked several large junks,
mounting from ten to fifteen guns each.

With these junks they formed a very formidable
fleet, and no small vessels could trade on the coast
with safety.   They plundered several small villages,
and exercised such wanton barbarity as struck horror
into the breasts of the Chinese.   To check these enor-
mities the government equipped a fleet of forty imperial war-junks, mounting from eighteen to twenty guns
each.   On the very first rencontre, twenty-eight of the
imperial junks struck to the pirates; the rest saved
themselves by a precipitate retreat.

These junks, fully equipped for war, were a great acquisition to them. Their numbers augmented so rapidly, that at the period of my captivity they were supposed to amount to near seventy thousand men, eight hundred large vessels, and nearly a thousand small ones, including row-boats. They were divided into five squadrons, distinguished by different coloured flags: each squadron commanded by an admiral, or chief; but all under the orders of A-juo-chay (Ching yǐh saou), their premier chief, a most daring and enterprising man, who went so far as to declare his intention of displacing the present Tartar family from the throne of China, and to restore the ancient Chinese dynasty.

This extraordinary character would have certainly shaken the foundation of the government, had he not been thwarted by the jealousy of the second in command, who declared his independence, and soon after surrendered to the mandarines with five hundred vessels, on promise of a pardon. Most of the inferior chiefs followed his example. A-juo-Chay (Ching yǐh saou) held out a few months longer, and at length surrendered with sixteen thousand men, on condition of a general pardon, and himself to be made a mandarine of distinction.

The Ladrones have no settled residence on shore, but live constantly in their vessels. The after-part is appropriated to the captain and his wives; he generally has five or six. With respect to conjugal rights they are religiously strict; no person is allowed to have a woman on board, unless married to her according to their laws. Every man is allowed a small berth, about four feet square, where he stows with his wife and family.

From the number of souls crowded in so small a space, it must naturally be supposed they are horridly dirty, which is evidently the case, and their vessels swarm with all kinds of vermin. Rats in particular, which they encourage to breed, and eat them as great delicacies;* in fact, there are very few creatures they will not eat. During our captivity we lived three weeks on caterpillars boiled with rice. They are much addicted to gambling, and spend all their leisure hours at cards and smoking opium.

* The Chinese in Canton only eat a particular sort of rat, which is very large and of a whitish colour.

THE END.

LONDON:
Printed by J. L. Cox, Great Queen Street,
Lincoln's Inn Fields.

THE

SUPPRESSION OF PIRACY

IN

THE CHINA SEA,

1849.

BY

ADMIRAL THE RIGHT HON.
SIR JOHN C. DALRYMPLE HAY, BART.,
K.C.B., D.C.L., F.R.S., &c., &c.

LONDON: EDWARD STANFORD,
26 & 27, COCKSPUR STREET, CHARING CROSS, S.W.
1889.

SUPPRESSION OF PIRACY

CHINA SEA,

1849.

AT all times piracy was known to be rife in the
China Sea. At various periods it has assumed
formidable proportions. In the sixteenth century
Manilla was threatened by one piratical fleet; in
the seventeenth century Formosa was conquered
from the Dutch by another. In 1808, another
chief was known to have collected eight hundred
armed junks and seventy thousand men. The
Chinese war navy, never powerful, was helpless
before these freebooters. It generally endeavoured
to restore order on its seas by the payment of
black mail, or by offering large bribes to the
pirate chiefs, and, if possible, enlisting them in
the Government service.

The coast of China is covered from the Canton
River to the Min by a fringe of islands. Innumerable channels give ready access to excellent
anchorages, which, thanks to the admirable sur-
veys of Captains Collinson and Kellett, are now
accurately known. It is frequented by countless

fishermen, who are hardy boatmen, and who do
not scruple to add the business of wreckers, of
smugglers, or of pirates, to their more legitimate
calling.

When the China War ended, in 1842, the duty
of the British Navy in those seas was restricted
to the protection and encouragement of legitimate trade.   At the five Treaty Ports—Canton,
Amoy, Foochafoo, Ningpo, and Shanghai—con-
sulates were established, and a man-of-war was
stationed, to support the consular authority and
afford the requisite protection to our ships and
commerce.   At various other ports along the sea-
board, the great mercantile houses of Jardine,
Matheson, and of Dent, anchored their receiving
ships.   Opium, which is one of the products of
British India, from which it derives a large
revenue, was contraband.   China afforded the only
market for its sale.   The mercantile houses named
had the requisite capital to purchase the drug at
Malwa, Benares, and Patna, and the means to
distribute it profitably in the only sure market—
the Chinese.

The Chinese authorities and people had a great
desire for opium and a great dislike to the
foreigners who supplied it ; but in those years
they had not yet established its cultivation, and
were obliged to bear with the traders who supplied
their wants, in spite of their hatred of these
persons.   Large tracts of country in China are

now scarlet with the poppy, and China may soon be able to supply its own requirements by native produce. The Indian monopoly then required that the consuls and captains should display a benevolent blindness to those engaged in this traffic, and should afford without regard to person or property, the necessary protection to British subjects. Opium and other goods were sold on the deck of the receiving ship to native purchasers and distributed through China by their means. Junks, singly or in fleets, bore merchandise, both legal and illegal, all along the coast, and much of it, tea and silk as exports, and innumerable British products as imports, were continually carried coastwise between Singapore and the Hoangho.

In 1843 and 1844 the depredations of the marauders on British trade carried in Chinese bottoms, had caused some of the consuls to direct the attention of their naval colleagues to the importance of putting a stop to piracy. Some piratical junks were captured and their crews handed over to the Chinese mandarins at Amoy and the Min with the approbation of these authorities. But at Canton the jealousy of the Chinese authorities made them deprecate foreign interference in protecting their shores.

While Keying remained Imperial Commissioner no remonstrance was offered; but when Seu succeeded him he made strong representations to the Governor of Hong Kong to suspend or prevent any naval interference. In consequence the British Government directed its Commander-in-chief to issue the following order :—

"*Agincourt*, Hong-Kong,
18*th May*, 1844.

"In consequence of a representation I have received from H.E. Sir Henry Pottinger, it is my direction Her Majesty's ships and vessels, as well as those of the Indian service employed on the coast of China, do not interfere directly or indirectly with any ship, vessel, or boat, they may fall in with, belonging to Chinese subjects, under the supposition that he may be a pirate, or have been engaged in any unlawful act, unless he shall have within view attacked some British vessel or subject (or that on such proof of the fact that would satisfy a Court of Admiralty in England); in which case only, the said vessel is to be detained or interfered with.

"(Signed)   Thomas Cochrane,
Admiral and Commr -in-chief."

This order was subsequently amended on the 8th March, 1845, by omitting the clause in brackets and substituting " that the proofs are so strong of her having molested a British vessel as to leave no doubt of that fact."

This order, for which Sir Thomas Cochrane was unjustly blamed, was issued by order of the

Ministry at home. It checked the consular action in endeavouring to find evidence for invoking British naval assistance, and it deterred naval officers from undertaking a duty for which they were more likely to be blamed than thanked. In consequence, piracy rapidly increased in China. In Borneo prompt measures undertaken by Sir Thomas Cochrane, Sir James Brooke, and Captains Keppel and Farquhar had extirpated the pirates along its north-west shore, and similar success would have attended the same officers in China had they not been prevented by orders from home. The force which cleared the Sakarran and Serebas rivers and brought Sheriff Housman to condign punishment at Malludu Bay would have been equally successful in protecting our trade in China had it been permitted to do so. The depredations of the pirates increased in audacity, when they found that the Chinese navy dared not, and the British navy would not use its force against them. The Chinese traders in despair hired armed Portuguese lorchas to accompany their fleets, and considerable sums were spent in hiring this description of convoy. Occasional opportunities arose in which the proof seemed sufficient to justify capture, but frequently, though morally certain of the character of the junk, no overt act such as the order contemplated could be proved. Indeed, for a time it was only when a convoy protected by lorchas had been attacked and the depositions of the European captain of the lorcha could be obtained, that captains of the Queen's ships thought themselves justified in making prizes of the piratical junks, which they would, but for the order, have apprehended.

As an example, on the 14th November, 1846, the Governor of Hong Kong informed the Commander-in-chief that a piratical junk had anchored in the Lymoon. The *Wolverine*, Commander Dalrymple Hay, was at once despatched to support the police gunboat which was sent to search her. The junk was at anchor with many others. The first searched was a fishing junk, and no overt act could be brought home to any of them. When dawn broke on the 15th the pirate weighed and beat up to Shelter Bay, where she joined thirteen more, like herself, armed. In the bay also were two Chinese war junks, so that the *Wolverine* had to leave the duty of bringing these pirates to justice to the Mandarins, which they failed to do. Hay's conduct was approved. Soon after, Sir Thomas Cochrane returned to England from his successful command. He represented that the order prevented the navy being as useful as it might be in protecting trade in China. It was not even then repealed. More active measures were, however, contemplated by the Admiralty. During 1848 the squadron in China had to lament the death of Admiral Inglefield, who fell a victim to climate before he had been able to investigate

affairs in China. It was not till 1849 that
Admiral Sir Francis Collier succeeded him, and
he, as soon as he had made inquiry, obtained the
repeal of the order. It was full time. The
audacity of the pirates knew no bounds.

On 31st May, 1848, the *Columbine*, Commander
Dalrymple Hay, and *Scout*, Commander F. E.
Johnstone, proceeded in search of some piratical
junks near Amoy, and the *Scout* captured two of
them. The Chinese authorities at Amoy were
entirely satisfied, and the pirates condemned.

On the 7th June, the *Columbine* and *Scout* again
proceeded in company to search for pirates, but
although some were seen, no overt act could be
proved to justify their capture. The pirates, however, rapidly increased, and various occasions
arose when they might have been attacked but for
the unfortunate order.

On the 23rd August, 1848, the *Columbine* was
lying at the Taepan Islands, the outer anchorage
of Amoy. The barometer was falling and a
British brig, the *Hector*, came and anchored outside the islands in a dangerous position. Hay
sent an officer on board with an offer to assist in
moving the *Hector* to a safer anchorage. Mr.
Flockhart, the master, refused to be advised or to
move. As the gale increased and darkness came
on, it became evident that the *Hector* could not
ride out the gale. Hay, therefore, caused a stream
anchor and cable to be put into his pinnace, and

at three in the morning proceeded in the direction in which the *Hector* must have drifted. At early dawn the *Hector* was seen inside the shoals and breakers, over which she had been driven, and beyond were seen a large fleet of Chinese pirates. The gig having outstripped the pinnace, soon approached the *Hector*. Her reefed sails were loose, and she was still drifting with an anchor down. Alongside her were numerous large sampans, the boats of the pirate fleet. To wait for the pinnace would have been fatal. Any hesitation would have displayed weakness. The gig's crew were told to see their cutlasses free. Thomas Cook, the bowman, was desired to jump on board and make fast the painter to the starboard aftermost fore shroud. David Stenhouse, the coxswain, and Henry Nicholson were ordered to slip if possible and make sail. Richard Connell went aft to the wheel. The gig pushed in through the boats, who in the dim morning could not see whether she was supported by others. The gig's painter was made fast. Hay, Lieutenant Lyon, and the four men jumped on board. Mr. Flockhart dropped on his knees in gratitude. The anchor was tripped and sail was made. The *Hector* glided away from the crowd of Chinese boats before they knew what was about to happen. The *Hector* was 100 yards away when a frantic yell from the boats showed their rage and disappointment. Hay's knowledge as a pilot enabled him to navigate her through the shoals, and by noon the *Hector* was safe at anchor beside the *Columbine*.

This occurrence revealed the fact of a large piratical fleet close to Amoy. The before mentioned order had not been repealed, and no steps could be taken to attack and destroy them.

On the 3rd of December, 1848, a messenger came overland from Foochafoo to Amoy from Johnstone to say that the *Scout* was wrecked in the river Min. Hay, as it was the height of the north-east monsoon, decided on beating up under the lee of the islands which fringe the coast. This he succeeded in doing under treble-reefed topsails and reefed courses in fourteen days. He was thus able to ascertain that the pirate fleet which usually sheltered there had left the neighbourhood of Amoy. On arriving in the Min, H.M.S. *Medea* had also arrived. Commander Mason, the senior officer, had accidentally put into the Min, but was to proceed forthwith on other service. The *Scout* was then lying with thirty feet of water over her at high water, and with her forefoot resting on a rock at the most picturesque and dangerous part of this beautiful river. Mason and his officers had decided that the *Scout* was hopelessly wrecked. They had commenced to take the masts out and to empty her of stores with a view of abandoning her. Upon a careful examination of her position and consultation with Johnstone, Hay came to a different conclusion. As the senior officer at Amoy and the Min he expressed this opinion to Mason, who yielded to his representations. The *Medea* left, and after six weeks' strenuous exertions on the part of Johnstone and the officers and crews of the *Columbine* and *Scout*, they had the satisfaction of raising the *Scout*, replacing her masts and stores, and sending her to Hong Kong, where she saluted Sir Francis Collier's flag on the 20th February, 1849, and returned safely to England after completing her term of service in China.

Meantime the pirate fleet had run down to Bias Bay, and in its inner waters Shap'n'gtzai, the pirate chief, had his dockyard. It was to the outer roadstead of this port that the *Wolverine* in 1846 had chased the rover before alluded to. Emboldened by impunity, and within fifty miles of Hong Kong, Shap'n'gtzai had established relations with many of the Hong Kong traders. Near Stanley on the south side of the island is the Chinese village of Wongmakok.

On Sunday, 25th February, 1849, Captain d'Acosta of the Royal Engineers, and Lieutenant Dwyer of the Ceylon Rifles, who were stationed at Stanley, left at four in the afternoon for a walk. They were accompanied by Lieutenant Grantham and Dr. Tweddel of the Ceylon Rifles, but the two last named turned back before reaching Wongmakok. At mess d'Acosta and Dwyer were absent. They were never seen again alive, but the body of poor d'Acosta was found on the sea-shore on Tuesday the 27th February. It was afterwards ascertained that these two officers had been murdered by Chuiapoo, the second in command of the pirate fleet, then lying in Bias Bay. It was found that Wongmakok was the port through which European civilisation was able to supply the wants of the pirates.

Between Macao and the Bogue is the Cumsing-moon anchorage. This was outside the boundary of the port of Hong Kong. It was a sort of No Man's Land, in which neither Mandarin law, nor Portuguese law, nor Consular writ would run. In it were anchored the receiving ships both of British and American mercantile firms, and thither came to be supplied with opium and gunpowder, both lawful and unlawful traders. Among the ships at that time moored there, were the British ships, *Lady Hayes*, Captain George Lungley, the *Bombay*, Captain Charles Jamieson, and the United States ship *Ruparell*, Captain Endacott. There lived sometimes on board the *Ruparell*, and sometimes on board her own fast boat, as the mistress of Captain Endacott, a handsome, rich, and clever Chinese named Aku. She had amassed a considerable fortune by trade, which she prosecuted with much intelligence and daring—also without any scruples of conscience, of which it may be said she had none. Aku was the principal agent by whom Shap'n'gtzai's fleet was provided, and her own evidence as well as that of Captain Lungley and Jamieson given at Hong Kong on the 23rd September, 1849, revealed the relations in which she stood to the pirates.

In 1849 the Governor of Macao was Captain d'Amaral of the Portuguese Navy, who had served with Sir Charles Napier in the Miguelite war. He was straightforward, abrupt, and fearless, well-disposed to England and heartily anxious to put down piracy in China. On the 9th June the *Mœander*, Captain Hon. H. Keppel, then senior officer in China, and the *Amazon*, Captain Troubridge, were at anchor at Macao. A regatta was to take place there. Keppel and Troubridge having visited Canton were returning to Macao for the regatta, and Keppel desired Hay, then in the *Columbine* at Whampoa, to take them down to their ships. On arrival, invitations were found, inviting Keppel and Troubridge to dine at Government House. But before dinner Keppel became aware of an incident which led to tragic results. A considerable concourse from Hong Kong and Canton had assembled at Macao for the regatta. Amongst others a young Protestant missionary named Summers had landed to see the town. Whilst walking on the Praya Grande the Host was carried past. The Portuguese, both at Goa and Macao, are scrupulously Catholic in their outward respect to this sacred emblem. Native and foreigner uncovered as it passed, but Mr. Summers stood defiantly with his hat on. The crowd were incensed and a riot seemed probable. The police in the interests of order arrested Mr. Summers.

As this was going on, the Governor, who happened to be passing, and saw at a glance what had occurred, rode up to Mr. Summers, and said, "Take off your hat, man; if you will not take it off to the Host, take it off to me. I am the Governor." Mr. Summers did not choose to avail himself of this loophole, but insisted on being a martyr, and the Governor was perforce compelled to allow the police to apprehend him.

Mr. Summers was thrown into jail to await an examination before a magistrate next day, for obstruction and causing a riot. The Governor had no power to control the civil magistrate, and his good-natured intervention having proved fruitless, he was obliged to allow the law to take its course. When Keppel landed to dine with the Governor, he was greatly incensed that a British subject, who had come over for a holiday, should have been thrown into prison, for not taking his hat off to Host or Governor, and perhaps had not sufficiently considered that the law, and not the Governor was in fault. Before dinner he requested to see the Governor in private with Troubridge, and demanded Mr. Summers' release. The Governor replied that he was powerless in the matter, and that he had done his best to save

Mr. Summers' conscientious scruples, by telling him
to take his hat off to the Governor, if he would not
take it off to the Host. To this Keppel replied,
" Have you heard of William Tell and his answer
when ordered to uncover to Gessler?" The
Governor made no reply then, but after dinner,
having communicated with the magistrate who
committed Summers, he leaned over the balusters
as Keppel descended the staircase and said, "My
dear Keppel, I will let the fellow out, to oblige
you." To which Keppel replied, "I am not going
to accept as a favour what I have demanded as a
right." The next morning orders were issued at
daylight by Keppel to the *Amazon* and the
Columbine to send their boats, manned and armed,
to the steamer lying in Macao harbour, which was
to serve as a rendezvous, and as a stand for the
judges at the regatta.

The boats came, the arms were piled on the
steamer's deck, the marines were drawn up there,
and every one supposed these arrangements were
only a part of the day's amusements. The boats
had shared in various races which occurred before
noon, and at noon it was proposed to suspend the
races for an hour, that the crews might dine, and
the spectators lunch. Then Keppel called Troubridge to him and said, "Man and arm the
boats; land at once; take a party of men and a
powder bag; go up to the jail, blow in the door,
and bring Mr. Summers out. I place Hay under

your orders, to protect your boats and communications." The boats landed, Hay lined the beach at the back of the parapet which bounds the Praya Grande with his marines and seamen. Troubridge and his party rushed up the street to the jail, blew in the door, and brought out Mr. Summers. Meanwhile the Portuguese guard had lined the Praya Grande on the opposite side to the marines, and loaded their muskets. At the sound of the explosion the Portuguese troops came to the ready. Past them came clattering Troubridge and his men with Mr. Summers. The heavy guns were trained upon the British ships, and everything portended bloodshed. But Troubridge had done his work so quickly, that Mr. Summers was in the gig on his way to the *Columbine*, the marines and seamen had been re-embarked, and the races recommenced before a shot was fired. The episode seemed to have vanished like a dream.

Not so, however, in its effects. The pirates, emboldened by the seeming difference between their enemies the British and the Portuguese, encroached upon the Portuguese territory, and the luckless Governor riding outside the gates, was assassinated on the 22nd August, and beheaded by the desperadoes, a part of whose fleet had established itself at St. John's and Tienpak. Keppel left the China station for South America. Troubridge became senior officer in China, and Hay, after landing

C

Mr. Summers at Hong Kong, returned in the *Columbine* to his station at Whampoa. M. Jurien de la Gravière, in the 'Revue des deux Mondes,' in an article entitled "d'Amaral et les pirates Chinoises," has related these proceedings with candour and impartiality.

After this, the activity of the pirates increased. The main fleet, under Shap'n'gtzai, consisting of over seventy sail, had their rendezvous at Tienpakh, and ravaged the coast and preyed on the traders from Macao to the Gulf of Tongkin. The second division, under Chuiapoo, had their rendezvous at Bias Bay, and carried on the war from Hong Kong to Amoy with about forty sail of well-found, well-armed junks.

On the 30th April, Commander Hoseason, in the *Inflexible*, was sent to examine the Lemma Islands for pirates who had recently made a raid in Hong Kong harbour. As the ship approached, the pirates opened fire on the *Inflexible* at about 1200 yards' range, but the superior gunnery of the British soon silenced the fire, and the boats under Lieut. Gordon were sent to bring the junks out. Six were taken, their crews deserting to the shore.

On board one of the junks was found the property of M. Pages, of Signor Orense, and other persons lately missing. M. Pages had been Secretary to the French Legation, and with Signor Orense had been murdered just before when attacked by pirates on their voyage from Hong Kong to Macao.

In May, June, and July, Commander Lyons, of the *Pilot*, was able to capture or destroy ten piratical junks and 252 pirates. The skill with which he conducted the three several enterprises, in all of which he succeeded, was most marked, and was an earnest of the future career of that distinguished officer whose heroic death at Sebastopol, almost in the presence of his father, Sir Edmund Lyons, was so tragic in its circumstances, and shed such a gloom over the Black Sea fleet.

In May, while at anchor off the Min, a Portuguese lorcha, waiting for a convoy, was attacked by pirates. On the 13th May, the *Pilot* chased six of them, and captured and destroyed two with her boats. On the 25th May, Lyons captured and destroyed one off Meichow, and on the 27th another. On the 2nd June, at Goochakang, one more was destroyed, and on the 3rd another, so that only one of the six escaped. On the 20th June, the *Pilot* again, three more of Chuiapoo's squadron having been reported, succeeded in destroying one in Red Bay on the 25th June, and one off the Lamyat Islands. In these operations the *Pilot* had one man dangerously and two slightly wounded. The Governor of Amoy was much gratified, and expressed his warm thanks to Lyons for the protection thus afforded, as did the Chinese Admiral, who had been unable to give that protection to commerce which was so much required. In consequence of these operations, the Amoy division of Shap'n'gtzai's fleet went down the coast to Bias Bay.

On the 28th July, a salt-boat, lying close to the *Minden* in Hong Kong harbour, was cut out, and news was brought to Hong Kong that the *Sylph*, *Greyhound*, *Coquette*, and *Anne Eliza*, which had sailed from Hong Kong for Singapore, were all missing. The *Sylph* had much treasure on board, and the *Medea*, now commanded by Commander Lockyer, was sent down the coast by Troubridge to examine it in search of those missing ships.

On reaching Tienpakh, on the morning of the 7th September, Lockyer found the inner harbour completely filled with fifty heavily armed junks. The mandarin had retreated into the country for fear of the pirates, and upwards of one hundred peaceful trading junks were detained in the harbour by the pirates until payment was made by way of ransom. Lockyer went into the harbour in his gig; a division of five junks were despatched to endeavour to cut him off, and for this purpose anchored in a creek near the mouth of the harbour. Lockyer, however, boarded one of the junks, where they were received with civility and entertained at tea. After tea Aku presented herself, stating that all these armed junks were pirates. She was there, poor, innocent lady, endeavouring, she said, to persuade Shap'n'gtzai to release some of her goods on board the traders he had detained, but really was engaged in supplying the pirate fleet, and buying from them the spoil they had seized from the trading vessels. Lockyer, however, having seen no overt deed of piracy against a British ship, was unable to act. He proceeded on his voyage to search for the *Sylph*. In leaving the bay Lockyer boarded a junk outside. This junk stated that her companion had British goods on board, and had been seized by the pirate fleet.

Fortified with this excuse, Lockyer returned, manned and armed his boats, and proceeded, guided by the junk captains who had given the information, to search for the junk with British goods. In rowing into the harbour, the five pirate junks detached in the creek opened fire upon the *Medea's* boats. Lockyer then gave orders to return the fire and board, and in the short space of half-an-hour most gallantly captured them. He had one man killed, and Mr. Wilkinson, Sergeant Henwood, and seven men wounded. The main body of the fleet was observed to be getting under weigh to cut off the boats. So Lockyer set the five captured junks on fire and returned to his ship. The *Medea* drew too much water to enter the harbour; the fleet was obviously too powerful to be attacked by the boats alone, so Lockyer, having done all that skill and courage could achieve, went on in search of the *Sylph*.

The search proved unsuccessful, and the *Medea*

returned to Hong Kong. Lockyer was thence ordered to Whampoa, on the 10th September, to relieve the *Columbine*, where six of the pirate fleet which he had seen at Tienpakh shortly after anchored. He gave information to the Chinese authorities at Canton, but this necessary delay enabled the pirates to sail, and they then escaped capture. On the 28th September, however, five war junks were sent by the Chinese Government to capture them. The pirates captured the Chinese admiral and all five junks off the Lemma, put their crews to death, carried the mandarins and officers on shore, kindled a fire, and roasted them alive.

Meanwhile, on the 8th September, Lieutenant Mould, first lieutenant of the *Amazon*, had been sent by Troubridge from Hong Kong in the merchant steamer *Canton*, which had been chartered by the mercantile and insurance houses at Hong Kong, to search for the missing ships. Mould took with him some seamen and marines from the *Amazon* whom Troubridge had sent to assist in this duty.

On the 8th September, Mould, in the *Canton*, commanded by Charles Jamieson, proceeded to Macao, and thence, on the 9th, to St. John's. On that day a pirate junk was captured and burnt, and her prize, a salt-junk, was released. At 2.30 that afternoon the *Canton* boarded a junk laden with sugar, which had just been released from Tienpakh by Shap'n'gtzai for 1100 dollars ransom. At 11.30 p.m. the *Canton*

passed through a fleet of junks, which was afterwards ascertained to be the pirate fleet. On the
10th, at 3 a.m., the *Canton* anchored at Tienpakh. Two boats were sent in to examine three
junks which remained in the port. On approach-
ing the nearest, the boats were received with a
heavy discharge of firearms, stinkpots, and spears,
and several men were wounded. The two boats
returned to the *Canton*, and at daylight she entered
the harbour and approached the three pirates. On
this the pirates entered their boats and endeavoured
to escape. The *Canton* intercepted them, and but
few reached the shore alive. Eleven prisoners
were taken. The three junks, of which the largest
mounted nineteen guns, were burnt. The prisoners
stated that Shap'n'gtzai, whose flags and papers
were found on board, had sailed with the fleet on
the previous evening.

The *Canton* followed to Nowchow. There it
was found Shap'n'gtzai had stripped the Chinese
fort of its guns in passing, and had proceeded to
Hoi-how, in Hainan. Mould there made the ac-
quaintance of Hwang, who was subordinate to Ho,
the Governor-General of Hainan, also a Chinese
naval mandarin. Hwang was in command of the
ten war junks stationed at Hoi-how. Shap'n'gtzai
had attempted to levy black mail, and had sent
some of the lighter vessels up the river for this
purpose. Hwang had attacked them and destroyed
two, but his fleet had lost two of his own junks

in the action, and he himself had been wounded. He had beaten off the pirates, however, who had gone on into the Gulf of Tonkin.

The people were very friendly when Mould, Captains Jamieson and Soames, and Messrs. Olding and Bowring visited the authorities. On the 12th Hwang returned the visit.

On the 13th September the *Canton* fell in with four more of the pirate fleet off Mamee, and drove two of them ashore and destroyed them. The Teipo of Mamee expressed his thanks for this assistance. This day, however, was one on which a typhoon of great violence blew. The *Canton* put into Mamee Bay where she rode it out in safety; one of the *Amazon's* boats was wrecked. Her crew were saved and well treated by the inhabitants and authorities, who readily recognised the valuable services being rendered in delivering them from the scourge of piracy. On the 15th the *Canton* returned to Hong Kong, and Mould and his men to the *Amazon*.

During the typhoon of the 13th, the *Columbine* was anchored in Anson's Bay, outside the Bogue Forts. On the 14th, she joined the *Amazon* at Hong Kong, and was desired to prepare for her return voyage to England.

Troubridge had been desired to join the Admiral at Singapore, leaving Hay temporarily senior officer at Hong Kong. On the return of the *Canton*, Troubridge decided that an effort should be made to destroy any of the pirate fleet which might still be in the neighbourhood of Macao, St. John's, or Mamec.

He therefore ordered Hay to take the *Phlegethon*, which had arrived with the *Amazon's* boats and men, and search that part of the coast. This duty was performed between the 19th and 21st September. At Sahto it was found that some of the pirate fleet had been wrecked in the typhoon of the 13th and 14th, but none were seen. On returning to Hong Kong, Troubridge determined to examine some of the suspected harbours himself on his way to Singapore. The *Amazon* sailed on the 23rd accompanied by the *Phlegethon*. They found the various ports empty, and the *Phlegethon* returned to Hong Kong and Canton on the 26th.

Before sailing Troubridge desired Hay to run over in the *Columbine* on the 21st to Macao, and to put himself in communication with Commodore Geisinger of the United States Navy, who was at anchor there in the *Plymouth*. On arrival Hay was told by the Commodore that he had been informed by Captain Endacott that some piratical vessels had been seen in the Cumsingmoon, and had seized some American cargoes. Commodore Geisinger had therefore sent the United States schooner *Dolphin*, with his first Lieutenant Thomas Jefferson Page, and a strong force. They had seized the two junks in question and had brought them to Macao. Governor d'Amaral

would not receive them, and Commodore Geisinger was anxious that the pirates should be
tried in the Admiralty Court at Hong Kong.
Hay accordingly received the junks from the
American Commodore, and putting Mr. Douglas
Walker in charge of one and Mr. C. R. Goddard
in the other with prize crews, desired them to
follow to Hong Kong. The *Columbine* returned
there on the 24th with Walker's prize, and
Hay found himself senior officer.   Governor
Bonham approved of the step which Hay had
taken in assisting the Americans to try their
piratical prizes. As Goddard was sailing over at
nightfall, he was attacked by other piratical junks
and with excellent judgment bore up and took
refuge under the guns of the *Plymouth*, whither
his assailants did not follow him.   Commodore
Geisinger sent Captain Gedney on board, and he
arranged with Goddard to send an officer and
some United States seamen to assist him.   The
junk thus additionally protected reached Hong
Kong in safety on the 26th.

The trial took place on the 4th October,
and evidence was given before the court which
proved the piracy and incidentally gave the clue
to much information.   Before the trial eight
more suspicious junks were captured in the
Cumsingmoon by the *Plymouth*. Aku herself
came before the court and gave evidence. Lieutenant Page, now a distinguished Admiral in the

Argentine service, and Lieutenant Fox, afterwards Under-Secretary of the Navy at Washington, added much information, and the history of Shap'n'gtzai and of Chuiapoo was made public. Aku proved that the two first junks handed over to the British were her property; that she had gone to Tienpakh to see Shap'n'gtzai (where she was met by Lockyer as already related) to reclaim her opium and cargoes confiscated by him and held to ransom; that she had persuaded him to repay her, and that having sold the opium he had stolen from her, he had recompensed her by handing over the two junks in question with British goods on board, which had been taken from some of the captured ships.

Shap'n'gtzai, or Chang-shih-wu-tz, who had raised himself to be the chief of this formidable force, was living at Hong Kong in 1845. He was now between 30 and 40 years of age, tall, with a sharp chin, long upper lip, clean shaven, very dark in complexion, aquiline nose, large dark eyes, and slightly marked with smallpox. Seu, the Viceroy of Quantung, demanded his extradition. It was refused by Sir John Davis, and he continued to live under the British flag till 1846. Tzeeapo (Chuiapoo) at the same time was living at Victoria as a barber—it has since been thought with the view of obtaining good information and eventually cutting throats in a more congenial manner. His murder of d'Acosta and Dwyer obliged him to

leave Hong Kong, and he was soon joined to
Shap'n'gtzai as his second in command.

Shap'n'gtzai, although willing to possess the
support of so able a second in command, brooked
no rival.

Another pirate named Lo had commenced business on his own account. Shap'n'gtzai attacked
him, captured his ships, and put him to a cruel
death. After this deed he was, in the month of
September, in treaty with Seu to be received with
his fleet into the Chinese navy, and to be appointed to clear the seas of pirates. The terms he
demanded were considered too high, and it remained for the British navy to rid the sea of this
pest in a more legitimate manner.

On the 27th September Governor Bonham informed Hay that he had received intelligence by
an escaped fishing-boat that Chuiapoo was ravaging the coast about 90 miles to the eastward of
Hong Kong. The *Phlegethon* was at Canton, the
Hastings, though hourly expected from Singapore,
had not arrived, and the *Fury*, Commander James
Willcox, which had just arrived, was not ready, so
Hay decided to proceed with the *Columbine* alone in
the direction indicated. The wind was light and
the water smooth as on that afternoon the *Columbine*
swept through the Lymoon Pass. On the 28th she
reached Harlaem Bay and found that Chuiapoo had
burnt Pinghoi, a village there which had refused to
contribute a ransom. A merchant and a fisherman

of Pinghoi were on board the *Columbine*. They
had escaped by carrying a boat across the neck
of land near Fokai Point, as the pirates then
had blockaded the harbour, and had brought the
information to Governor Bonham on which Hay
was now acting. The fishermen there indicated
Tysami as the direction in which he had gone.
At 11 p.m. the *Columbine* was off Tysami, which
was observed in flames, and by the light of a
bright clear moon, fourteen junks, formed in two
lines, were seen sailing off to the south-west. The
Columbine gradually closed with them, and passing
between the two lines hailed the leading junk of
the starboard line to heave to and send a boat on
board. All this time the breeze which was failing
just enabled the pirates to keep station under sail,
and the *Columbine* to manœuvre so as to avoid
being boarded by them. The junks refused to
heave to, gongs and drums announced their determination to fight, stinkpots were triced up, ready
to throw on board, so the *Columbine* poured three
well-directed broadsides into their leader. This
was quickly returned, and the breeze falling, the
Columbine had again to betake herself to her
sweeps. Once she was deliberately raked, and
fourteen shot holes were left in the foot of the
mainsail. The men having secured themselves in
time at quarters, no one was wounded, and by
three in the morning of the 29th the pirates
finding they had caught a tartar, made off by

sweeping to the south-west. The *Columbine* followed
by the same means. Three of the junks which had
suffered most in the night action, were abandoned,
and their crews were seen to be distributed in the
remaining eleven. About noon the pirate fleet
was observed to be in some confusion, altering
course towards the shore. Soon a steamer was
observed coming from the westward, round Fokai
Point. This proved to be the *Canton*, on this
occasion chartered on behalf of Mr. Watkins, a
citizen of the United States, to search for the
Coquette, a missing vessel. Captain Jamieson at
once, with the full and ready consent of the gallant
American, steamed for the pirates, and then seeing
that they were too powerful for his ship, closed the
Columbine and towed her into action. The *Canton*
being badly damaged by a shot through her steam-
chest, was at last obliged to cast off the *Columbine*.
Ten of the pirate junks made off for Harlaem Bay,
the one nearest to the *Columbine* sailed into a creek
in the shore to the eastward of Fokai Point, where
behind a rocky promontory she was lost to view.
No chart existing of this creek, the *Columbine*
essaying to enter, grounded. Hay immediately
signalled the *Canton* to come to his assistance,
and a tow rope being sent on board, she was towed
out of her perilous position. While the ship was
still aground the pinnace, cutter, and gig were
sent in under Lieutenant Bridges, to cut out the
junk. He was accompanied by the brave Watkins,

who insisted on volunteering. Soon the sound of firing was heard. A Chinese fort with two guns joined in the fray, too glad to have an opportunity of destroying a pirate while assisted by the British boats. The pirate fought with desperation. At last Bridges boarded, followed by the gallant Charles Goddard. The pirates fled over the bows into boats, but one desperado, seizing a lighted joss-stick, ran down below. Goddard divining his intention, rushed after him sword in hand, but before he could overtake him the rogue had fired the magazine, and the junk was blown up. Poor Goddard was thrown into the sea and picked up much scorched and he died the next day, a splendid example of a high-spirited and gallant English gentleman. The pirate being destroyed, Bridges returned. In addition to Goddard, three men had been killed and six wounded in the attack.

On the return of the boats it was calm, and the *Canton* towed the *Columbine* through Harlaem Bay to the entrance of Bias Bay, where they anchored. Early next day, Sunday, 30th September, Hay sent the *Canton* to Hong Kong with the wounded, and Goddard who died on the passage. About 3 p.m. the *Canton* anchored near the *Hastings*. Watkins delivered Hay's despatch to the Commander-in-chief. Admiral Sir Francis Collier lost no time in ordering the *Fury* with a strong detachment of seamen and marines, commanded by Lieutenant Luard, to go to the assistance of the *Columbine*.

About 1 a.m. on Monday, 1st October, the *Fury* joined the *Columbine*. At daylight the *Fury* towed the *Columbine* up through the channels in Bias Bay, and from time to time gained information from fishermen as to the pirate's haunt. At the north-eastern corner of Bias Bay is a long tortuous creek called Fanlokong or the Ram's-horn. The *Columbine* was anchored at the mouth of this, and the *Fury*, preceded by Hay in his boat sounding, slowly steamed up it. As the last turn in the creek opened, behind a rocky promontory fifteen junks were seen in line. They at once opened fire upon the *Fury*, about 10 a.m. This solved all doubt, if there were any. The *Fury* returned the fire. Thirty-two shot penetrated her, but only one man was wounded. Her excellent practice crippled one after another of the pirates. In forty-five minutes their fire was almost silenced. When quite so, the boats of the two ships went in, and under cover of an occasional shell, completed the destruction. By half-past four twenty-three piratical junks, three new junks on the stocks, and many stores in their dockyard called Typoon had been destroyed. Above 200 guns were captured, Hay having landed with a force of seamen and marines, drove the pirates off, while the boats completed the destruction.

On the return of the *Columbine* and *Fury* to Hongkong, Sir Francis Collier desired Hay to prepare to conduct an expedition in the *Columbine*

to the eastward to endeavour to destroy Shap'n'g-
tzai's fleet, as he had already destroyed Chuiapoo's.
The *Fury* and *Phlegethon* were placed under his
orders, and he was given *carte blanche* as to time
and place of search. At 9 a.m. on the 8th October
the three ships sailed from Hong Kong. The 9th
they reached St. John's, and there fell in with another of the junks released from Tienpakh before
Shap'n gtzai sailed for Hoihow. On the 10th
they anchored at Mong, and on the 11th at
Mamee, looked in to Tienpakh, and finding it
empty arrived at Nowchow on the 12th. Here
the pilots confirmed Lieutenant Mould's report.
No ships of the draught of the *Columbine* or *Fury*
had ever passed through these inner waters before.
But the squadron was successfully carried through
the 60 miles of unknown and hidden dangers, and
anchored off Hoihow at 3 p.m. on Saturday, 13th
October. Hay immediately landed, and was
received by Hwang, who informed him that he
was just about to put to sea in search of some of
the pirates. He had been slightly wounded in
the late engagement, but was ready for work.
He said, however, that he must obtain orders to
associate himself with the British from Ho, the
Governor-General of Hainan. For that purpose
Hay and Willcox, accompanied by other officers,
proceeded to Kienchue, the capital. They were
received by Ho most hospitably.

The centre gates were opened and an illumi-

D

nated garden had been prepared to do honour to
the guests. Ho had also served as a naval mandarin, and upon Hay offering to embark Hwang
and his staff on board the *Fury*, readily assented.
On Sunday, 14th October, boats came off with presents of roast pigs, fowls, ducks, kids, vegetables,
and fresh beef for each ship's company, from the
Governor-General.

At noon, Hwang with his secretary and aide-de-
camp embarked on board the *Fury*, desiring his
eight junks, if they could not keep company, to
rendezvous at Gueichow; for he recognised the
necessity of quick movements, lest Shap'n'gtzai
should receive notice of the approach of the
squadron. The eight junks were not seen again,
but the fact of their being associated with the
squadron gave its acts the benefit of the approval
of the Chinese Government. On the 15th the
squadron anchored in the splendid anchorage on
the south side of Gueichow Island. Curiously
enough, Hwang visited the temple there and
informed us that the priests had assured Shap'n'g-
tzai that he would be in great danger on the 20th,
but that if that day passed without any evil
befalling him, he might look forward to a long and
prosperous career. Shap'n'gtzai had left this for
Pakhoi. On the 16th Pakhoi was reached, in the
north-east corner of the Gulf of Tongkin. Here
it was found he had burnt the village and gone
off to Chookshan in the north-west corner of the

Gulf, behind Cape Pahlung. On the 17th this too was searched, and it appeared that he had proceeded with his squadron into the unknown waters which form the archipelago in the north-western part of the Gulf of Tongkin. For this part of the world there was then neither chart nor sailing direction. Even now, the French, whose surveyors have for fifteen years been busily surveying it, in the chart for this year, say here are innumerable islands which are not yet laid down.

From Cape Pahlung to the delta of the Sang-kwa or Red River, for more than sixty miles, the Bay of Faitzilong is studded with thousands of rocks and islands, many of fantastic forms, some wooded and some bare, some low lying, and some elevated, in which it seemed almost hopeless to pursue the pirate fleet.

The Red River or Sangkwa enters the gulf by many mouths. At that time the Tonquin, which was the boundary between China and Cochin China, was supposed to be a separate river. It is now believed to be one of the mouths of the Sangkwa. The three mouths of the Tonquin are the Cua Nam Trou, the Cua Keum or Cua Cam, and the Cua Tray. Off these mouths are the Norway Islands of the old charts. Close into the mouths is the island of Cua Ba, about 700 feet high, which forms the end of the archipelago. The alluvial soil brought down by the Tongkin forms a shifting bar off the three mouths of the river, and inside it a long, deep lagoon receives the waters of all three before discharging them into the sea. It was inside this bar and at the mouth of the Cua Keum that Shap'n'gtzai had taken his fleet. Many creeks extend from one to the other and connect the three, whilst opportunity was afforded if hard pressed to slip out and evade pursuers in the archipelago. On the Cua Keum, about ten miles from the sea, was the Cochin Chinese town of Haiphong.

Fortunately for the British, Shap'n'gtzai had threatened Haiphong in order to obtain supplies, and the Cochin Chinese authorities were justly incensed and alarmed.

It was through the archipelago above described, that Hay conducted his squadron. The north-east monsoon was favourable, the water smooth and clear. The *Columbine* in the centre, with the *Fury* to her left and the *Phlegethon* to her right, wended her way at 7 or 8 knots an hour. At times the ships were in sight of each other, at others hidden behind the islands, but always within signal distance. They beat this archipelago as a covert, and by the time they had traversed about 30 miles, they feared that they had missed the object of their search.

On reaching Gowtoshan on the 18th October, a junk was seen in a creek almost hidden by trees. The *Columbine* and *Fury* anchored, and the *Phlegethon* went in and destroyed her. The crew fled inland, but one of them and a fisherman who was a prisoner were taken. From them, Hwang and Mr. Caldwell the interpreter found out that Shap'n'gtzai was about 12 miles off among the islands, and that the junk destroyed was his look-out ship. On the 19th the squadron passing Norway Island, anchored under Cua Ba and Hoonong. No news could be obtained. Then Hay took Willcox, Hwang, and Mr. Caldwell with him to reconnoitre in the *Phlegethon*. They heard from a fisherman that Shap'n'gtzai and a large fleet were at anchor in the Cua Keum, and that Haiphong was preparing to resist him. Early on the 20th Hay proceeded in the *Phlegethon* in the direction indicated. Soon they saw over the low islands the sails of many junks, some under-weigh and some at anchor, but it seemed impossible to discover a channel by which to approach them. The *Phlegethon* and the boats in vain attempted to find it. At last a fisherman from a neighbouring creek came out in his boat, and volunteered to show a channel.

When at Pakhoi one of Aku's fast boats had come down to communicate with Shap'n'gtzai. When he saw that his hiding-place had been dis-covered he charged the emissary with treachery, and the wretched man was lashed to the mast of the flagship, where he perished. A messenger also arrived from Seu, the Governor-General, with proposals as to the arrangement for acquiring

Shap'n'gtzai's services for the Chinese Government.
Him he beheaded also on suspicion of betraying
his refuge.

As the squadron approached the shore, it was
seen that twenty-seven of the fleet were anchored inshore of the banks and islands which lay
opposite to the Cua Keum. They were anchored
in a line slightly concave to the sea and river
mouth, and extending about a mile and a half,
with their heads to the north and springs on their
cables. The flagship of 42 guns was twelfth from
the van, and the other twenty-six seemed able to
show nine guns on the broadside. Two hundred
and sixty-four guns were therefore bearing on the
narrow entrance. They were anchored in close
order, and there was no room for more to anchor
in line at that anchorage. The islands and mud
flats were too wide to make it possible to shell
them from outside. They were too strong to be
attacked with the *Phlegethon* and boats alone, and
when the estuary in which they were anchored
was entered by the squadron, it was too narrow to
make it practicable to take advantage of accurate
fire from a distance.

About half-past four it was high water. The
Phlegethon, in which Hay was, led in. The *Fury*
with the *Columbine* in tow followed close in her
wake. As the *Phlegethon* got inside the bar, the
pirate fleet opened fire. Fortunately the tide had
just begun to ebb, and this brought an unlooked-for

advantage to the assailants. The strain came on
the springs of the pirates, and before they could
correct it the battle had begun. Thus it happened
that each pirate's broadside was directed across his
neighbour's stern, as they lay in a bow and quarter
line, with their heads to the north-west. So regular
was this that an eyewitness mistakenly reports
that Shap'n'gtzai fired on some of his own vessels,
for their negligence during the fight. Hay immediately seized this advantage. The *Columbine*
was anchored about 600 yards from the flagship's
quarter. Hay himself proceeded in the *Phlegethon* through the line and engaged and destroyed
the two rear ships, which were the only ones whose
guns could bear on the *Columbine*. He sent Willcox in the *Fury* to attack the van, which he most
judiciously did, choosing also a point of impunity.

After destroying the two ships above mentioned,
Hay proceeded in his boat to the *Fury*, for he
deemed it important to keep in touch with Hwang.
When he had rowed along the pirate line, which
frequently saluted him with shotted guns, he found
the *Fury* had destroyed four and was engaged with
the fifth from the van. Hwang was delighted,
success seemed assured, so Hay left Willcox to complete the good work he had so well begun. He proceeded to the *Columbine* to make arrangements for
the boats to complete the destruction at nightfall.
As he rowed down a splendid sight gratified the
squadron. Like *L'Orient* at the Nile, the flagship

was blown into the air. For a minute or two the fire slackened, then resumed with redoubled vigour. By-and-by the hull of the flagship, which still floated, burnt down to the hemp cables; they were set on fire and the flaming hull drifted down in the hawse of the *Columbine*. The *Phlegethon* was signalled to come and tow her out of her peril. Niblett gallantly pushed his ship between the bow of the *Columbine* and the flaming mass, which had already scorched the fore rigging of the *Columbine*. A tow rope was thrown on board and the *Phlegethon* towed the *Columbine* up the river to the place where the rear ship of the line had originally floated.

By this time it was dark, but all the twenty-seven were totally destroyed. Shap'n'gtzai had, however, saved himself, and the long low island between the Cua Keum and the Cua Nam Trou was covered with men who had landed from the burning vessels. In a creek about two miles up, which passed between the Cua Keum and Cua Nam Trou, were many of the pirate fleet, who had been too numerous to anchor with advantage in the battle of the 20th; other masts were seen in the Cua Tray. The squadron was therefore moved up so as to command the creek in question, as well as the Cua Tray and Cua Keum.

Sunday, the 21st October, Trafalgar day, commenced with far different feelings from those which had been experienced by the squadron only

twenty-four hours before. The long chase of
Shap'n'gtzai had then appeared fruitless, the toils
and perils of the navigation through which the
squadron had passed in safety were all again to
be encountered, and the results obtained seemed
worthless.

Now the squadron felt confidence in its commander, and the proud satisfaction of having
achieved a success of the greatest value to commerce. There were in sight thirty-nine more of
the pirate fleet, but scattered in various creeks
and in no group more than nine together. Moreover, the creeks were narrow, and in no place
could more than one vessel be moored broadside on.

The country people, though scared, were friendly,
but unless the remaining pirates were destroyed,
they could not be expected to take the part of the
British. It was Sunday morning ; a short service
was held and prayers for the victory and for
the personal protection vouchsafed were publicly
offered. Then arrangements were at once made
for attacking and destroying the remaining pirate
fleet. Hay in the *Phlegethon*, with the *Columbine's*
boats, proceeded up the Cua Tray. Lieutenant
George Hancock with the paddle-box boats of the
Fury proceeded up the creek opening from the
Cua Keum, while Willcox in the *Fury*, and Bridges
in the *Columbine*, remained in their respective
vessels to blockade the river at the point of junc-

tion of the creeks and prevent any escaping to sea
with the boats under their charge.

The *Phlegethon* in the Cua Tray destroyed
twenty. One only attempted to fight. The
Phlegethon steaming up the narrow creek in which
the pirates lay moored, watched them training the
stern gun upon her as she steamed up the tortuous
channel. As she approached, it was wondered
why the gun was not fired; when she was boarded,
the captain of the gun was found with others killed
by a lucky shell, with the lanyard in his hand,
and many a life in the *Phlegethon* may be said to
have been spared in consequence. However, that
" every bullet has its billet " is, perhaps, a truer
explanation. In the creek George Hancock succeeded in attacking with impunity nine, so huddled
together that when the first was taken the rest
followed. His skill and judgment were much
applauded. By nightfall, after a laborious day,
thirty more had been destroyed of the once famous
fleet of sixty-four vessels. On the 22nd, the Cochin
Chinese authorities from Haiphong came down
and expressed their gratitude. The pirates on
the islands, the wrecks, and the guns, were made
over to them.

On Tuesday, the 22nd, the squadron left for
Hoihow, and arrived on the 25th October. Ho
welcomed them most gratefully. He visited the
ships, and begged hard that they would stay.
But that was impossible. On Friday, the 26th,

the squadron sailed. It blew a gale from the north-east, and it was not possible on the 28th or 29th to cross the bar at Nowchow. On the 30th it was attempted again, and the *Fury* towed the *Columbine* over successfully. On Wednesday, the 1st November, the *Columbine* and *Fury* anchored in Hong Kong. The *Phlegethon* had been detached to give information at Tienpakh of Shap'n'gtzai's destruction. But the joy of the successful men and officers was sadly damped by the news that the gallant admiral, under whose auspices the expedition had sailed, and by whose wise arrangements it had triumphed, had passed away, and was not there to welcome them. Sir Francis Collier died on the 28th October. It was his encouragement which infused the enthusiastic spirit that made the China squadron in 1849 so successful. Hay, Willcox, Lyons, Bridges, Hancock, Chambers, Close, and Walker, were promoted. From longitude 115° E. to 104° E., over 1000 miles of perilous and unknown waters, they had tracked the pirates and completely destroyed them. The grateful merchants presented services of plate to the successful commanders, and for a time trade flowed smoothly, free from the perils which piracy had added to its usual risks.

But the chief credit due to the British officers was the manner in which they conciliated and gained the assistance and support of the officers of the United States Navy, the approval of the

French, Spanish, and Portuguese authorities, and the concurrence and active support of the Chinese Government and the Cochin Chinese officials—a unanimity without which such ample success would have been impossible, and which was as rare as it was beneficial to the interests of commerce.

LONDON : PRINTED BY EDWARD STANFORD, 26 & 27 COCKSPUR STREET, S.W.

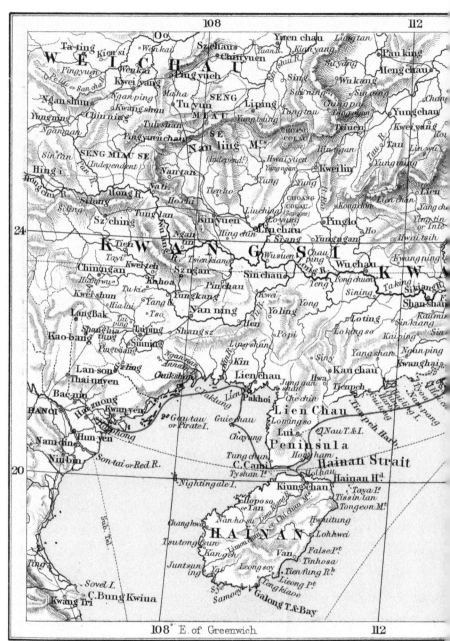

Oo

Ta-ting Kien-si Wenkai Szehaur Chinyuen Ymen chau Liugtan

WĒI CHAU Yuan R. Kiah yang Pau kang

Pingyuen Wenkai Sing Su-yang Wu-kang Heng chau

Kd d or San cha Kwei yang Pingyuch Sri shut R.

Nganshun Nganping Majha SENG Liping Sin ning Sin ning

Kwang shun Tu yun Tang tau Chingpa Tingsuen Yung chau

Yungning Chin ning MEU Yungtsung Tsiuen Kwei yang

Ngannan Tul shan SE COLA Kin ngan Tau Tan Lin wu

Ping yuei chau Nan ling M. Hwui yuen Yung ui ty

Sin Tan SENG MIAU SE Independ. Yungngan Kweilin

Hing i (Independent) Hwui yuen Yung Yung Lien chan Yang tin

Hong cha R. Siling Hong R. Van tan Yung Kongchin Yang tin or Lin tsih

Siting Ho di Tien ho CHOANG Lien Hwui tsih

Sz ching Tung lan Kin yuen Liuching Loying Pinglo Ho

24 Tien Hing chin Tu chau Shang Yungngan

Tayi R. Tsien kiang Wusuen Chau ping Wuchau Kwangning

Chinngan Kwei tch Sz ngan Sin chau Long R. Teng Tong chuen Sining Sikiang R. KWA

Hiangwu Tu kie Pin chau Hwei Yong Taking Shan shan

Kwei shun Hia lui Yang k Yungkang Yo ling Loting Kaunu

Lang Bak tai Tso Hen Sin kiang Kaiping Sin

Shan chia ping Taiping Shangsz Popi Lokingso Yang shan Nganping

Kao bang tung Simning Lingshan Sing Kwanghai

Pingtsiang Kin Yang shan Kwanghai

Lan son Sz ling Ngantran Annam Lien chau Hwa Kau chau Tienpeh

Thai nuyen Chuk shan Lien Pakhoi Jung uan Che chin Tien peh Tsin peh Harb Nan pang

Bac ninh Hai zuong Kwan yen Gou tau or Pirate I. Guie chau Lomingso Lien Chau Noak pang

HANOI Haiphong Chayang Lui Nau T. & I. Taya I.

Nam dinh Hun yen Tung chun Peninsula Hongham Hainan Strait

Niubin Son-tai or Red R. C. Cami Hoihau Hainan Hd

20 Nightingale I. Tyshan I. Kiungchan Taya Is.

Iloposo or Tan Tissin lan Tongeon Mt

Changhwa Nanho su Kimkiang R. Chi chau Hwuiting Lohkwei

Ting HAINAN Van False Pt

Tsutong sun Kan geh Limmon Leongsoy Tinhosa

Sovel I. Juntsun ing Yai Tien fung Rk Lieong Pt

Kwang Tri C. Bung Kwiua Samoey Tengkiaoe

Galong T. & Bay

London: Edwar

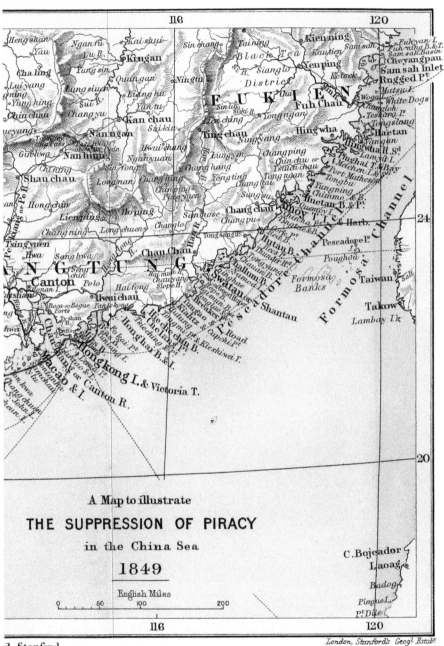

A Map to illustrate

THE SUPPRESSION OF PIRACY

in the China Sea

1849

English Miles

0   50   100   200

For EU product safety concerns, contact us at Calle de José Abascal, 56–1°, 28003 Madrid, Spain or eugpsr@cambridge.org.